بسم الله الرحمن الرحيم

First published 2004
© Goodword Books 2004

Goodword Books Pvt. Ltd.
1, Nizamuddin West Market
New Delhi-110 013
E-mail: info@goodwordbooks.com
Printed in India

ISBN 81-7898295-1

Translated by Suheyla B. Sarac

Abbreviations used:
(saas - *sall-Allahu 'alyahi wa sallam*):
May Allah bless him and grant him peace
(following a reference to the Prophet Muhammad)
(as - *'alayhi's-sallam*): Peace be upon him
(following a reference to the prophets or angels)

www.goodwordbooks.com

TRUE WISDOM DESCRIBED
IN THE
QURAN

They will say: "If only we had really
listened and used our reason, we would not
have been Companions of the Blaze."
(Surat al-Mulk: 10)

HARUN YAHYA

GOODWORD BOOKS

ABOUT THE AUTHOR

Now writing under the pen-name of HARUN YAHYA, he was born in Ankara in 1956. Having completed his primary and secondary education in Ankara, he studied arts at Istanbul's Mimar Sinan University and philosophy at Istanbul University. Since the 1980s, he has published many books on political, scientific, and faith-related issues. Harun Yahya is well-known as the author of important works disclosing the imposture of evolutionists, their invalid claims, and the dark liaisons between Darwinism and such bloody ideologies as fascism and communism.

His penname is a composite of the names *Harun* (Aaron) and *Yahya* (John), in memory of the two esteemed Prophets who fought against their people's lack of faith. The Prophet's seal on the his books' covers is symbolic and is linked to the their contents. It represents the Qur'an (the final scripture) and the Prophet Muhammad (peace be upon him), last of the prophets. Under the guidance of the Qur'an and the Sunnah (teachings of the Prophet), the author makes it his purpose to disprove each fundamental tenet of godless ideologies and to have the "last word," so as to completely silence the objections raised against religion. He uses the seal of the final Prophet, who attained ultimate wisdom and moral perfection, as a sign of his intention to offer the last word.

All of Harun Yahya's works share one single goal: to convey the Qur'an's message, encourage readers to consider basic faith-related issues such as Allah's Existence and Unity and the Hereafter; and to expose godless systems' feeble foundations and perverted ideologies.

Harun Yahya enjoys a wide readership in many countries, from India to America, England to Indonesia, Poland to Bosnia, and Spain to Brazil. Some of his books are available in English, French, German, Spanish, Italian, Portuguese, Urdu, Arabic, Albanian, Russian, Serbo-Croat (Bosnian), Polish, Malay, Uygur Turkish, and Indonesian.

Greatly appreciated all around the world, these works have been instrumental in many people recovering faith in Allah and gaining deeper insights into their faith. His books' wisdom and sincerity, together with a distinct style that's easy to understand, directly affect anyone who reads them. Those who seriously consider these books, can no longer advocate atheism or any other perverted ideology or materialistic philosophy, since these books are characterized by rapid effectiveness, definite results, and irrefutability. Even if they continue to do so, it will be only a sentimental insistence, since these books refute such ideologies from their very foundations. All contemporary movements of denial are now ideologically defeated, thanks to the books written by Harun Yahya.

This is no doubt a result of the Qur'an's wisdom and lucidity. The author modestly intends to serve as a means in humanity's search for Allah's right path. No material gain is sought in the publication of these works.

Those who encourage others to read these books, to open their minds and hearts and guide them to become more devoted servants of Allah, render an invaluable service.

Meanwhile, it would only be a waste of time and energy to propagate other books that create confusion in people's minds, lead them into ideological chaos, and that clearly have no strong and precise effects in removing the doubts in people's hearts, as also verified from previous experience. It is impossible for books devised to emphasize the author's literary power rather than the noble goal of saving people from loss of faith, to have such a great effect. Those who doubt this can readily see that the sole aim of Harun Yahya's books is to overcome disbelief and to disseminate the Qur'an's moral values. The success and impact of this service are manifested in the readers' conviction.

One point should be kept in mind: The main reason for the continuing cruelty, conflict, and other ordeals endured by the vast majority of people is the ideological prevalence of disbelief. This can be ended only with the ideological defeat of disbelief and by conveying the wonders of creation and Qur'anic morality so that people can live by it. Considering the state of the world today, leading into a downward spiral of violence, corruption and conflict, clearly this service must be provided speedily and effectively, or it may be too late.

In this effort, the books of Harun Yahya assume a leading role. By the will of Allah, these books will be a means through which people in the twentyfirst century will attain the peace, justice, and happiness promised in the Qur'an.

The works of the author include *The New Masonic Order, Judaism and Freemasonry, Global Freemasonry, The Kabbala and Freemasonry, The Knight Templars, Templars and Freemasonry, Israel's Policy of World Domination, Islam Denounces Terrorism, The Black Clan, Terrorism: The Ritual of the Devil, The Disasters Darwinism Brought to Humanity, Communism in Ambush, Fascism: The Bloody Ideology of Darwinism, The 'Secret Hand'in Bosnia, Holocaust Violence, Behind the Scenes of Terrorism, Israel's Kurdish Card, Communist China's Policy of Oppression in East Turkestan, Palestine, Solution: The Values of the Qur'an, The Winter of Islam and The Spring to Come, Islam and Buddhism, The Philosophy of Zionism, Articles 1-2-3, Romanticism: A Weapon of Satan, The Light of the Qur'an Has Destroyed Satanism, Signs From* the Chapter of the Cave in the Qur'an to the Last Times, The End Times and the Mahdi, Signs From the Qur'an, Signs of the Last Day, The Last Times and The Beast of the Earth, Truths 1-2, Idealism The Philosophy of Matrix and the True Nature of Matter, The Western World Turns to God, The Evolution Deceit, The Perfect Design in the Universe Is Not by Chance, Why Darwinism Is Incompatable with the Qur'an, Darwinism Refuted, New Research Demolishes Evolution, A Definitive Reply to Evolutionist Propaganda, The Quandary of Evolution I-II (Encyclopedic), The Error of the Evolution of Species, The Blunders of Evolutionists, The Collapse of the Theory of Evolution in 50 Steps, The Errors of The NAS: A Reply to the National Academy of Sciences Booklet Science and Creationism, Confessions of Evolutionists, Perished Nations, For Men of Understanding, Love of Allah, Allah's Art of Affection, The Glad Tidings of the Messiah, The Prophet Musa (as), The Prophet Yusuf (as), The Prophet Muhammad (saas), The Prophet Sulayman (as), The Prophet Ibrahim (as) and the Prophet Lut (as), Maryam (as) The Exemplary Muslim Woman, The Golden Age, Allah Exists, Allah's Artistry in Colour, Magnificence Everywhere, The Importance of the Evidences of Creation, The Truth of the Life of This World, The Nightmare of Disbelief, Knowing the Truth, Eternity Has Already Begun, Timelessness and the Reality of Fate, Matter: Another Name for Illusion, The Little Man in the Tower, Islam and Karma, The Dark Magic of Darwinism, The Religion of Darwinism, The Collapse of the Theory of Evolution in 20 Questions, Allah is Known Through Reason, The Qur'an Leads the Way to Science, Consciousness in the Cell, Biomimetics Technology Imitates Nature, The Engineering in Nature, A String of Miracles, The Creation of the Universe, Miracles of the Qur'an, The Design in Nature, Self-Sacrifice and Intelligent Behaviour Models in Animals, Deep Thinking, Never Plead Ignorance, The Green Miracle: Photosynthesis, The Miracle in the Cell, The Miracle in the Eye, The Miracle in the Spider, The Miracle in the Mosquito, The Miracle in the Ant, The Miracle of the Immune System, The Miracle of Creation in Plants, The Miracle in the Atom, The Miracle in the Honeybee, The Miracle of Seed, The Miracle of Hormones, The Miracle of the Termite, The Miracle of the Human Body, The Miracle of Human Creation, The Miracle of Protein, The Miracle of Smell and Taste, The Miracle of the Microworld, The Secrets of DNA, The Miracle in the Molecule, The Miracle of Creation in DNA, The Miracle of Talking Birds.

The author's childrens books are: Wonders of Allah's Creation, The World of Animals, The Glory in the Heavens, Wonderful Creatures, Let's Learn Our

Islam, The World of Our Little Friends: The Ants, Honeybees That Build Perfect Combs, Skillful Dam Constructors: Beavers, Tell Me About Creation, The Miracle in Our Body, A Day in the Life of a Muslim, Children This is for You I-II

The author's other works on Quranic topics include: The Basic Concepts in the Qur'an, The Moral Values of the Qur'an, Quick Grasp of Faith 1-2-3, Ever Thought About the Truth?, Crude Understanding of Disbelief, Devoted to Allah, Abandoning the Society of Ignorance, Paradise: The Believers' Real Home, Learning from the Qur'an, An Index to the Qur'an, Emigrating for the Cause of Allah, The Character of the Hypocrite in the Qur'an, The Secrets of the Hypocrite, Names of Allah, Communicating the Message and Disputing in the Qur'an, Answers from the Qur'an, Death Resurrection Hell, The Struggle of the Messengers, The Avowed Enemy of Man: Satan, The Greatest Slander: Idolatry, The Religion of the Ignorant, The Arrogance of Satan, Prayer in the Qur'an, The Theory of Evolution, The Importance of Conscience in the Qur'an, The Day of Resurrection, Never Forget, Commonly Disregarded Qur'anic Rulings, Human Characters in the Society of Ignorance, The Importance of Patience in the Qur'an, Perfected Faith, Before You Regret, Our Messengers Say, The Mercy of Believers, The Fear of Allah, Jesus Will Return, Beauties for Life in the Qur'an, A Bouquet of the Beauties of Allah 1-2-3-4, The Iniquity Called "Mockery," The Mystery of the Test, Real Wisdom Described in the Qur'an, The Struggle Against the Religion of Irreligion, The School of Yusuf, The Alliance of the Good, Slanders Spread Against Muslims Throughout History, The Importance of Following the Good Word, Why Do You Deceive Yourself?, Islam: The Religion of Ease, Zeal and Enthusiasm Described in the Qur'an, Seeing Good in All, How do the Unwise Interpret the Qur'an?, Some Secrets of the Qur'an, The Courage of Believers, Hopefulness in the Qur'an, Justice and Tolerance in the Qur'an, Basic Tenets of Islam, Those Who do not Heed the Qur'an, Taking the Qur'an as a Guide, A Lurking Threat: Heedlessness, Sincerity Described in the Qur'an, The Happiness of Believers, Those Who Exhaust Their Pleasures During Their Wordly Lives, A Sly Game of Satan, Passivism in Religion, The Religion of Worshipping People, Agonies of a Fake World, How a Muslim Speaks, The Silent Language of Evil, The Ruses of the Liar in the Qur'an, Loyalty in the Qur'an, The Solution to Secret Torments.

TO THE READER

* A special chapter is assigned to the collapse of the theory of evolution because this theory constitutes the basis of all anti-spiritual philosophies. Since Darwinism rejects the fact of creation—and therefore, Allah's Existence—over the last 140 years it has caused many people to abandon their faith or fall into doubt. It is therefore an imperative service, a very important duty to show everyone that this theory is a deception. Since some readers may find the chance to read only one of our book, we think it appropriate to devote a chapter to summarize this subject.

* All the author's books explain faith-related issues in light of Qur'anic verses, and invite readers to learn Allah's words and to live by them. All the subjects concerning Allah's verses are explained so as to leave no doubt or room for questions in the reader's mind. The books' sincere, plain, and fluent style ensure that everyone of every age and from every social group can easily understand them. Thanks to their effective, lucid narrative, they can be read at a one sitting. Even those who rigorously reject spirituality are influenced by the facts these books document and cannot refute the truthfulness of their contents.

* This and all the other books by the author can be read individually, or discussed in a group. Readers eager to profit from the books will find discussion very useful, letting them relate their reflections and experiences to one another.

* In addition, it will be a great service to Islam to contribute to the publication and reading of these books, written solely for the pleasure of Allah. The author's books are all extremely convincing. For this reason, to communicate true religion to others, one of the most effective methods is encouraging them to read these books.

* We hope the reader will look through the reviews of his other books at the back of this book. His rich source material on faith-related issues is very useful, and a pleasure to read.

* In these books, unlike some other books, you will not find the author's personal views, explanations based on dubious sources, styles that are unobservant of the respect and reverence due to sacred subjects, nor hopeless, pessimistic arguments that create doubts in the mind and deviations in the heart.

CONTENTS

INTRODUCTION

The human mind is vital for our existence and, in a sense, it is what makes us human beings. The ability to think profound thoughts, comprehend subtle issues, speak with wisdom, and differentiate right from wrong can be accomplished only with the power of our mind. Without a doubt there is no one on this earth who does not know the importance of these qualities. But there is a very important reality that many people don't know or fail to realize. Not everyone is as wise as people presume. Everyone has a certain amount of innate intelligence, but wisdom is a special capacity developed through specific conditions. These two notions, intelligence and wisdom, are usually perceived to mean the same thing by the general public. However, in the Qur'an the reality of the human status is summed up in the phrase: **"most of them lack wisdom"**. (Surat al-Ma'ida: 103)

Most people do not use their wisdom. So what is "wisdom"? How can the source of wisdom be reached? Who possesses real wisdom? Only the Qur'an gives us the right answers to these questions, because the Qur'an is Allah's word and it is the only source from which we can obtain absolutely accurate information on any topic. When we look at the Qur'an, we see that wisdom is only developed through having faith.

Anyone who turns toward Allah by listening to his conscience may possess this great blessing without exerting any physical effort. We only need to believe in Allah sincerely, fear Him as is proper, and lead the life our Creator wants us to. This sincere faith provides humans with wisdom. And this clear mind, with its influence over every moment of one's life, will lead to the right path.

This book will define the true meaning of wisdom. "What are the circumstances that bring about wisdom?", "Can wisdom increase or decrease?", "Can there be factors that cloud reasoning?", "If so, can they be removed?" Questions such as these and probably questions which most people will learn the real answers to for the first time will be answered. Everyone will be reminded once again how valuable a blessing the mind is.

Also, by drawing attention to examples of wiseness and unwiseness in the Qur'an, the clear distinction between the two will be portrayed. The great rewards, given in this world and the Hereafter, to the people of wisdom who obey the Qur'an will be explained. And the great losses experienced by those who don't use their minds and have strayed away from religion will be described: everyone will be exhorted to use his reason.

This book, as is expressed in Surat al-Muzzammil, verse 19: **"Let him who will take the right path to his Lord",** aims to open up a path for those who wish to draw near to Allah, comprehend His greatness, live by the morals of the Qur'an, and benefit from the blessings of our mind.

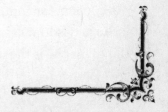

ABOUT WISDOM...

Wisdom has been variously defined throughout the ages. However, none of these numerous definitions have been enough to provide people with the real meaning of wisdom. This is because information seekers have not consulted an accurate source but tried to assess wisdom by their own reasoning. As we mentioned previously, the source from which we can get information on wisdom is the Qur'an, as revealed by Allah, Who possesses infinite wisdom.

Anyone who fears Allah and obeys the Qur'an is wise. However, most people are not aware that they can easily possess such a blessing. As they assume that wisdom is purely innate, they do not think it probable that they could acquire anymore than they already have.

For example, it is similar to a child believing that the world consists only of his house, his classroom, his teacher, and his toys. Obviously, it is not possible for the child to leave his little world and see the whole world with a mature pair of eyes. That is why all his ideals, his worries, and his activities are restricted to his own little world. Whereas, a mature adult, observing this child's life, can clearly see how restricted the child's world is. This is because the adult possesses the experience and knowledge that the world does not consist of just a house, a classroom, and a couple of toys.

So, a similar comparison can be applied to wisdom. A person lacking wisdom assumes that he knows the truth about everything, that he is the wisest person, and lives the most wonderful life. As a result, he believes that he treads the most righteous path. As he sees no possibility of leading a better life, a better way of thinking, he cannot compare and realize the difference. Whereas in the Qur'an, the gift of wisdom is mentioned as a great blessing which provides a superior way of life, the ability to comprehend greater issues, and thinking capability. So, this book will define wisdom according to the Qur'an and show that wisdom presents us with a clear consciousness and the ability to comprehend. In one of the verses Allah commands:

This is a warning to mankind. Let them take heed and know that He is but One Allah. Let the people of understanding bear this in mind. (Surah Ibrahim: 52)*

WHAT IS REAL WISDOM?

As we mentioned at the beginning of the book, the word "wisdom" in society is generally used to mean a person's level of intelligence. However, wisdom is a greater and a more profound way of understanding than innate intelligence is.

Intelligence, as is most commonly defined, is the sum of the human being's ability to think, perceive realities, and reach conclusions. The ability to adapt to first-time or suddenly encountered situations, to understand, learn, and analyse, the

---

* *The concept of "people of understanding" which appears in the English translations of the verse is a translation of the Arabic ulul albab, which literally means "possessors of wisdom" or "those who see into the core of a thing" (albab is the plural of lubb which also means "the core of a thing"). It is generally agreed in commentaries that this concept expresses a deep intelligence and conceptual ability. That is why it appears in the form "people of understanding" here.*

development of the five senses, concentration, thought, and attention to detail are all made possible through our intelligence. For example, an intelligent professor can promptly comprehend how things function physically and formulate it. Or an intelligent person with a good memory can understand intricate and detailed aspects of situations. And one with practical intelligence can come up with practical and simplified solutions to the situations he faces.

On the other hand, the wise man, as well as making use of the advantages intelligence provides, makes use of the comprehension and ability an intelligent person doesn't possess.

An intelligent person can only accomplish things with the knowledge and experience he acquires by examining particular topics or by otherwise educating himself. But, these are abilities such as depend on learning, memorizing, and experience. As a result, he may reach an impasse at some point, unable to find solutions to problems and carry things through to a satisfactory conclusion.

On the other hand, a wise person, without former education or experience, can reach more appropriate and definite conclusions on any given subject, which he has in fact never previously encountered than one who has studied that subject for many years. This is because, a wise person can find the most practical solution, even if he doesn't have any technical knowledge on the subject. If necessary, he can even apply to the person with the most experience on the subject to do the job and reach a solution. In brief, wisdom is an ability that provides us with greater comprehension than intelligence, deeper understanding, ability to find the truth, and produce a solution for every problem. Furthermore, wisdom is a trait that gives us control of all aspects of our lives and brings us success.

The sole attribute that endows us with this quality is faith. Allah gives special understanding to those who have faith and fear Him. In the Qur'an, the understanding awarded to those who fear Allah is explained thus:

> **You who believe! If you heed Allah, He will give you a criterion [by which to judge between right and wrong] and will cleanse you of your sins and forgive you. Allah's favour is indeed immense. (Surat al-Anfal: 29)**

As can be seen, wisdom comes about moment by moment as Allah reveals the truth to those who have faith and abide by their conscience. This attribute faith has endowed us with, gives us the ability to differentiate right from wrong and think correctly, make sound judgements, and reach the most sensible decisions in every part of our lives. A wise person can see details in situations that most people fail to see, distinguish subtleties, and arrive at the most accurate and sound conclusions. He or she can be farsighted concerning long-range plans, determine situations that may be encountered in the future, and devise flawless plans. In the same way, he makes the best use of his past experiences, drawing upon them wisely where most needed. Because he can evaluate events clearly, everything he does is beneficial, everything he says has wisdom, and his every reaction is ideal.

Moreover, wisdom forms a deeper meaning in the human soul, which allows us to derive more pleasure from the blessings of life. For this reason, people of wisdom can see the inner beauty of things which most people would regard as ordinary.

However, it is not possible to limit the definition of wisdom, since, wisdom is a privilege and an entitlement to superiority that affects every part of our lives. The information given in the following pages, will allow the reader to better comprehend the blessings gained from the wisdom acquired through faith.

THE REAL POSSESSOR OF WISDOM IS ALLAH

Human beings have been created. As a result, the wisdom seen in human beings is not an inherent ability; it has been given to them. The real possessor of wisdom is the Creator of human beings: Allah. Allah possesses infinite and unlimited intelligence and He gives intelligence whenever and to whomever He wills, in relation to the faith of the individual.

People who are given this blessing can evaluate their world in more subtle ways. Whichever corner of the universe they look at, they can see that every detail they encounter is full of examples of Allah's infinite intelligence. In the Qur'an, the helplessness of human beings in the face of Allah's superior intelligence and artistry is described with an example in the following verses:

> **He created the seven heavens one above the other. You will not find any flaw in the creation of the All-Merciful. Look again—do you see any gaps? Then look again and again. Your sight will return to you dazzled and exhausted! (Surat al-Mulk: 3-4)**

As the verses clarify, there is not the slightest deficiency in Allah's creation. Every faultless system encountered in the universe is an indicator of His superior intelligence. One reason why Allah displays to mankind such perfect systems is for human beings to know the real possessor of wisdom, to comprehend Allah's greatness, and to have faith in Him by submitting to Him.

The verse **"They said, 'Glory be to You! We have no knowl-**

edge except what You have taught us. You are the All-Knowing, the All-Wise'". (Surat al-Baqara: 32) in the Qur'an conveys the utterance befitting the wise who appreciate that Allah is the possessor of real wisdom.

WISDOM AND CONSCIENCE

As we mentioned in the previous chapters, anyone who follows his conscience can easily distinguish right from wrong. But there are those who try to suppress their conscience, even though they can hear it and know that it is telling them the truth. Eventually in this situation, people who don't listen to their conscience become unable to distinguish right from wrong. They don't think of Allah's greatness and their own vulnerability; they assume that they have acquired the qualities Allah has given them all by themselves and they become haughty.

For the sake of argument, let's take a scientist who has discovered the unknown secrets of space or the human body with the intelligence and skill Allah has given him. If this scientist doesn't use his wisdom, doesn't think of who created this faultless order in the universe and the human body, he cannot possess real conscience and comprehension. Instead of appreciating the perfection in the phenomenon he has discovered and turning towards Allah and praising Him, he becomes proud of himself and seeks admiration. In the Qur'an Allah tells us that such people who take their whims and desires to be their god have their hearts sealed as a result:

Have you seen him who takes his whims and desires to be his god—whom Allah has misguided knowingly, sealing up his hearing and his heart and placing a blindfold over his eyes? Who then will guide him after

Allah? So will you not pay heed? (Surat al-Jathiyya: 23)

As the verse declares, the one who becomes conceited by taking his own self as his god can no longer comprehend what he sees and hears. As a result of this, he will be deprived of a great blessing, such as wisdom.

As another example, let's take the researcher who has discovered the unmatched designs in nature and the faultless systems of living things. If this researcher claims that the things he witnesses are a result of chance, he will be greatly mistaken. And to say that this person is wise would be impossible. Because, wisdom is the ability to comprehend that the perfection in animate things and in systems is Allah's creation.

Such clever people may be in the spotlight with their inventions, knowledge, and skill and gain others' approval, give admirable speeches and achieve a superior position in communities far from religion. But, this is all on the surface; the reality is that such people cannot show any signs of real wisdom.

But it is also important to realise that these people are not aware of the position they are in. They suppose that their intelligence has brought them to the highest possible level and they become proud. But the wise can clearly see that such people are lacking in real wisdom. And they comprehend how powerless such people are in the face of Allah, regardless of what they may think. Allah thus explains the helpless situation of people who cannot think:

The unbelievers are like beasts which, call out to them as one may, can hear nothing but a cry and a call. Deaf, dumb and blind, they understand nothing. (Surat al-Baqara: 171)

DOES WISDOM INCREASE?

There is another distinction between intelligence and wisdom.

Wisdom is not something fixed. On the contrary it is an ability that can increase and develop throughout one's life. This characteristic of wisdom is directly related to fear and awareness of Allah and obedience to one's conscience. In following verse Allah commands believers to fear Him and take heed as much as they can: **"Fear Allah, with all your hearts, and be attentive, obedient and charitable."** (Surat at-Taghabun: 16) For this reason, no one should see his fear of Allah as sufficient: He should always seek ways to bring himself closer to Allah and strictly abide by his conscience.

Allah can then increase his comprehension and his ability to discriminate right from wrong, in relation to his sincerity and the serious effort he makes to gain His approval. This is Allah's support for those who believe and an important secret of the Qur'an. The individual can use this opportunity in the best way possible to acquire the blessings wisdom has to offer in this world and the Hereafter.

CAN WISDOM BE IMITATED?

One who has intelligence can recognize the superiority of someone who has wisdom and admire that person openly or secretly. He tries to imitate this wise person and to achieve the same superiority. But as he cannot appreciate that it is wisdom that gives him this uniqueness, he searches for the solution in the wrong place. He begins to observe this person's behaviour, conversations, and mannerisms and he tries to conduct himself likewise. He may read a library-full of books, increase his knowledge, good manners, and skills but he still cannot achieve the admiration and respect that this person has gained. This is because, the source of wisdom is not knowledge, skill, culture, or education. Of course, a wise person possesses these qualities and uses them in the most useful ways. But the real source of wisdom is faith; therefore, one who has no sincere faith in Allah can never achieve the superiority of wisdom whatever he does, neither by imitation nor in any other way.

Also, wisdom is not limited to specific manners used only at certain times. On the contrary, it is a quality of perfection that changes according to circumstances, conditions and situations. The man of faith shows clear insight in situations he never expected or in fact never encountered before, as well as in situations he encounters every day.

It is not possible for people who lack wisdom to imitate such perfection. They usually panic in situations they are experiencing for the first time, they don't know what to do, or cannot hit on the right thing to do, and usually end up without a solution. Such people do not possess the qualities that wisdom brings such as speed, quick-wittedness, ability to solve problems, and dynamism.

In the Qur'an, Allah mentions people who try to present themselves as religious and want to associate themselves with believers, even though they have no faith. These people, hypocrites as Allah calls them, can imitate certain qualities of the believers. For example, they may pray as Allah orders, may give alms, or preach religious sermons. Allah refers to the ostentation of their behaviour in the following verses:

> ... **Those who spend their wealth to show off to people, not believing in Allah and the Last Day... (Surat an-Nisa': 38)**
>
> **Hypocrites think they deceive Allah, but He is deceiving them. When they rise to pray, they do so lazily,**

showing off to people, and only remembering Allah a very little. (Surat an-Nisa': 142)
When you see them, their outward form appeals to you, and if they speak, you listen to what they say. But they are like propped-up planks of wood... (Surat al-Munafiqun: 4)

As can be seen, the reason such people perform some of the requirements of religion is to show off. But the reality is, these people cannot entirely imitate the behaviour of the wise. It becomes obvious that they are not sincere Muslims by the things they say and the reactions they make to situations quite unwittingly. Wisdom, therefore, is an important indicator that enables us to distinguish true believers from those who only try to profit the image of the faithful.

Allah's Messenger (saas) also related the following about the superficial morality of the hypocrites and warned Muslims to be on their guard against them: *"Do not be like the hypocrite who, when he talks, tells lies; when he makes a promise, breaks it; and when he is trusted, proves dishonest."* (Bukhari and Muslim)

WISDOM PAVES THE WAY TO REALITY

Wisdom is "a higher dimension of consciousness", which many people who have not attained faith have not experienced. With such consciousness the individual's mind is very clear. However, what provides this clearness is neither the brain's capacity, nor sharpness of intelligence, nor skill. The cause of this clearness of mind is the person's faith in Allah and the Qur'an. One who uses the Qur'an as a guide is rid of all the incorrect information he formerly had. This is replaced solely with correct knowledge.

Foremost among the knowledge he acquires, is the real meaning of this world. One with a clear mind knows from the Qur'an that Allah has created this world as a transient place to test humankind. He can clearly see that the world has been created attractive and adorned with pretty things on purpose, and that some people lose themselves among these things and forget their true life, which is the Hereafter. But the believer himself, as he can arrive at the reality of any situation through the Qur'an, prepares for the Hereafter.

It is the wise who can truly grasp the truth about death. A person with wisdom, even though he may be the richest, the most attractive, and the most esteemed, knows that being so will not be of any help to him when he dies one day. But, he also realizes that death is not an end but rather a beginning. People who lead their lives according to Allah's will will go to Heaven and those who get carried away with worldly life and forget their responsibilities toward Allah will end up in Hell. Furthermore, he recognizes that Heaven is infinite and far superior to this life which does not exceed 80-90 years and is full of shortcomings. For this reason, he sees death as the beginning of an infinite life where he will be united with Allah's mercy, rather than as an annihilation that brings sadness. This knowledge also allows him to fully comprehend the reality of the Hereafter.

Something else these people with the clear conscience stemming from wisdom can comprehend is the reality of fate. They know that Allah, the possessor of infinite wisdom, has created everything on earth, small or big, with a purpose and divine reason. Even if they face an event, which at first sight seems unfavourable, they never forget that every cloud has a silver lining and that Allah is merely testing them. Because they can grasp this reality, they submit to Allah with all their heart, they trust Him completely, and they gladly accept their destiny.

WISDOM PROVIDES RIGHT THINKING

The ability to think is an important characteristic of human beings. However, many people do not use this ability in connection with reasonable or useful issues. Instead, they apply it to issues that are not beneficial either to themselves or to others. Sometimes they think for hours at a time or even days on end, but even after spending so much time they cannot produce any solutions. However, for anyone to assert that he can think advantageously, he needs to be able to make positive use of his hearing, perception, and thoughts.

The wise person is different from others in that he does not think just for the sake of thinking. He thinks to arrive at a solution, to be of some help, to find the truth, and to produce beneficial results. He determines what he is supposed to think with his wisdom. He doesn't occupy his mind with things that will waste his time and not lead him to any solutions. For example, he doesn't worry himself with unfounded suspicions, Satan's deceitful whisperings, or waste his time with concerns for the future.

He uses the Qur'an as his guide in such matters and he bases his thoughts on issues on which Allah encourages people to reflect. Foremost on his list of topics, is to think of the almightiness of Allah Who created him, all others and all the things he knows. A wise person never fails to remember that Allah is not bounded by time and place, that His presence encompasses everything, that when every creature is dependent on Him, He is beyond need of any being, He is the owner and sovereign of the universe, He sees all creatures every second of their existence, He knows whatever they say, do, or whatever passes through their minds, and that He keeps the record of everything from the beginning of time till the end of it. Our Prophet (saas) has thus explained this clearness of the mind of the believers: *"There is a polish for everything that takes away rust; and the polish for the heart is the remembrance of Allah."* (Bukhari)

One of the things the wise think of the most is how to achieve Allah's love and approval, because, he knows that he is more responsible to Allah than to anyone or anything in the world. At every moment of his life and every event he faces he thinks of what would be the conduct that would best bring him close to Allah. He always uses his mind to do beneficial and good things, to behave in the best manner possible to others around him, to say the best words, and live by the morals approved of by Allah. By trying to meticulously follow the commands and restrictions set forth in the Qur'an, he spends all his energy to on being one of the people most loved by Allah.

Such people, who think by using their wisdom, are stated to have reached the most righteous and correct way by acknowledging Allah's greatness. This is elaborated upon in the following verses:

> **Those who remember Allah, standing, sitting and lying on their sides, and reflect on the creation of the heavens and the earth [saying]: "Our Lord, You have not created this for nothing. Glory be to You! So safeguard us from the punishment of the Fire." (Surah Al 'Imran: 191)**
>
> **In the creation of the heavens and earth, and the alternation of the night and day, and the ships which sail**

the seas to people's benefit, and the water which Allah sends down from the sky—by which He brings the earth to life when it was dead and scatters about on it creatures of every kind—and the varying direction of the winds, and the clouds subservient between heaven and earth, there are Signs for people who use their reason. (Surat al-Baqara: 164)

By thinking such things as bring benefit, one's wisdom is increased and he can thus act with much more insight. One who uses his reason encourages the people around him to act in a better way, as well as ensuring for himself great rewards in this world and the Hereafter.

ACCORDING TO THE QUR'AN, TO WHAT KIND OF TOPICS SHOULD HUMAN BEINGS APPLY THEIR WISDOM?

This is explained in detail in the following verses:

And in your creation and all the creatures He has spread about there are Signs for true believers. And in the alternation of night and day and the provision Allah sends down from the sky, bringing the earth to life by it after it has died, and in the marshalling of the winds, there are Signs for people who use their reason. (Surat al-Jathiyya: 4-5)

Allah sends down water from the sky and by it brings the dead earth back to life. There is certainly a Sign in that for prudent people. There is instruction for you in cattle too. From the contents of their bellies, from between the dung and blood, We give you pure milk to drink, easy for drinkers to swallow. And from the fruit

of the date palm and the grapevine you derive both in-
toxicants and wholesome food. There is certainly a
Sign in that for people who use their reason. (Surat an-
Nahl: 65-67)

In the earth there are diverse regions side by side: and
vineyards and cornfields, and palm-trees sharing one
root and others with individual roots, all watered with
the same water. Yet We make some things better to eat
than others. There are Signs in that for people who use
their reason. (Surat ar-Ra'd: 4)

Among His Signs are the creation of the heavens and
earth and the variety of your languages and colours.
There are certainly Signs in that for every being.
Among His Signs are your sleep by night and your
seeking after His bounty by day. There are certainly
Signs in that for all mankind. Yet another of His Signs
is the lightning, a source of fear and eager hope. He
sends down water from the sky, bringing the dead
earth back to life by it. There are certainly Signs in that
for people who use their reason. (Surat ar-Rum: 22-24)

It is He Who sends down water from the sky. From it
you drink and from it come the shrubs among which
you graze your herds. And by it He makes crops grow
for you and olives and dates and grapes and fruit of
every kind. There is certainly a Sign in that for people
who reflect. He has made night and day subservient to
you, and the sun and moon and stars, all subject to His
command. There are certainly Signs in that for people
who use their reason. (Surat an-Nahl: 10-12)

It was He Who dispersed you about the earth and you

will be gathered to Him. It is He Who ordains life and death and He Who alternates the night and day. So will you not use your reason? (Surat al-Mu'minun: 79-80)

He has made an example for you from among yourselves. Do you have any partners for what We have provided you with among those whom your right hands control? Do you [feel] the same in such a case so that you fear [these servants] just as you fear one another? In that way We make Our Signs clear for people who use their reason. (Surat ar-Rum: 28)

Did I not chase you, tribe of Adam, never to worship Satan, who truly is an outright enemy to you, but to worship Me? That was surely the right path. Yet he has led huge numbers of you into error. Why did you not use your reason? (Surah Ya Sin: 60-62)

It was He Who created you from earth, then from a drop of sperm, then from an alaq [embryo], then He brings you out as infants into the world, you may achieve full manhood, then decline into old age—though some of you may die before that time—so that you may reach a predetermined age and grow in wisdom. (Surah Ghafir: 67)

Those who obey to their Lord will receive the best. But as for those who disobey Him, even if they owned everything on the earth and the same again with it, they would gladly offer it as their ransom. They will receive an evil Reckoning. Their abode will be Hell. What an evil resting-place! Is he who knows that what has been sent down to you from your Lord is the truth like him who is blind? It is only the wise who pay heed. (Surat ar-Ra'd: 18-19)

What of him who spends the night hours in prayer, prostrating himself or standing up, mindful of the Hereafter, hoping for the mercy of his Lord? Say: "Are they equal—the wise and the ignorant?" It is only the wise who pay heed. (Surat az-Zumar: 9)

Do you not see that Allah sends down water from the sky which penetrates the earth to emerge as springs and then by it brings forth crops of varying colours, which then wither and you see them turning yellow and then He makes them into broken stubble? There is a reminder in that for people of understanding. (Surat az-Zumar: 21)

He gives wisdom to whoever He wills and he who has been given wisdom has been given a great good. But no one pays heed but people of understanding. (Surat al-Baqara: 269)

It is He Who sent down the Book to you from Him: chapters containing clear judgements—they are the core of the Book—and others which are open to interpretation. Those with disbelief in their hearts follow what is open to interpretation, desiring conflict, by seeking its inner meaning. No one knows its inner meaning but Allah. Those firmly grounded in knowledge say, "We believe in it. All of it is from our Lord". But only people of understanding pay heed. (Surah Al 'Imran: 7)

You who believe! Do not make friends with any but your own people. They will do anything to harm you. They love what causes you distress. Their hatred is evident from their utterances, but what their breasts hide is far worse. We have made Our Signs clear to you, if you will use reason. (Surah Al 'Imran: 118)

Say: "Come and I will recite to you what your Lord has made binding upon you: that you serve no other gods besides Him; that you shall be good to your parents; that you shall not kill your children because of poverty—We will provide for you and them; that you shall not commit foul sins, whether openly or in secret; that you shall not kill any person, for Allah has forbidden this—except for a just cause. That is what He instructs you to do, so that, hopefully, you will grow in wisdom. (Surat al-An'am: 151)

We sent apostles before you but mortals inspired by Our will and chosen from among the people of the cities. Have they not travelled the land and seen the final fate of those who disbelieved before them? The abode of the Hereafter is better for those who guard against evil. So will you not use your reason? (Surah Yusuf: 109)

When Our Messengers came to Lut, he was distressed on their account, feeling incapable of protecting them. They said, "Do not fear and do not grieve. We are going to rescue you and your family—except for your wife; she will be one of those who stay behind. We will bring down on the inhabitants of this city a devastating punishment from heaven because of their deviance." We have left a Clear Sign of them behind for people who use their reason. (Surat al-'Ankabut: 33-35)

WHAT WISDOM BRINGS WITH IT

The wise are defined in the Qur'an as: **"Those who listen well to My precepts and follow the best in them are the ones whom Allah has guided. They are the people of understanding"**. (Surat az-Zumar: 18) Allah had rewarded these people with wisdom because, they unfailingly follow the path Allah has shown them, they carry out the advice of the Qur'an meticulously, and they clearly abide by their conscience.

Wisdom is a very important factor that opens the doors to many other beneficial qualities. A wise person displays his uniqueness in every situation, by his actions, and the things he says, and he elicits great respect and admiration from those around him. Wisdom is such an important quality, that it goes on making one more and more superior right to the end of one's life.

The pages to follow will be a reminder of what a blessing wisdom is by touching on some examples of the superiority conferred by wisdom.

GOOD MANNERS

Foremost among the qualities people of wisdom acquire is the morality of the Qur'an, which opens the paths to many beauties in this world and the Hereafter. The wise man is one who meticulously practices the morals Allah lays down in the Qur'an. The Qur'an recommends such moral qualities as honesty, genuineness, sincerity, modesty, peacefulness, compassion, justness, tolerance, and forgiveness among many other virtues. And a wise person is successful in displaying all of these qualities in the best possible way, in every situation he or she faces. He knows that the more care he takes in evincing these qualities, the better Allah will recompense him in the Hereafter.

For this reason, a wise person acts according to his conscience in situations he faces every day. For example, he helps someone in need without leaving the responsibility to others. He carries out all the good things he knows that Allah will approve of, without missing any of them. Or he helps someone who is trying to carry a heavy object instead of sitting and watching him. Whenever he sees someone who is elderly or sick on a bus, he prefers to stand and give his seat to that person. Otherwise he knows that he will be uncaring and this is something Allah will not approve of. Even when he faces a situation that angers him, he knows that Allah will prefer him to act with kindness, so he overcomes his anger and responds to the person concerned with kind words. He is always honest, even when he knows that it will be of disadvantage to him.

One, who displays all the above qualities in the best possible way till the end of his life using the full power of his mind, lives a good life in this world. Moreover, because he was aiming to please Allah with his behaviour, he will be rewarded with Heaven are elaborated upon in the following verses:

> **But as for those who believe and do right actions, We will not let the wage of good-doers go to waste. They will have Gardens of Eden with rivers flowing under them. They will be adorned in them with bracelets made of gold and wear green garments made of the finest silk and rich brocade, reclining there on couches**

under canopies. What an excellent reward! What a wonderful repose! (Surat al-Kahf: 30-31)

SAGACITY – DISCERNMENT

Sagacity is the human ability to understand and comprehend things quickly. Discernment is the ability to recognize the essence of things, to be foresighted and to have an insight on the truth in its every detail. The source that provides both these qualities to human beings is their wisdom.

In one of His verses, Allah draws attention to the importance of discernment and defines people who lack this quality as blind; **"The blind and the seeing are not the same. Nor are those who believe and do right actions the same as evildoers. What little heed they pay!"** (Surah Ghafir: 58)

In another verse in the Quran, the difference between those who possess this quality through wisdom and those whose sight and comprehension are blocked is compared as:

Is he who knows that the truth has been sent down to you from your Lord like him who is blind? It is only people of understanding who pay heed. (Surat ar-Ra'd: 19)

One who possesses sagacity and discernment has the capability to analyse an event, a behaviour, or a word in the best possible way. He can draw the best conclusions from his past experiences and use these in the most appropriate way for future events. He can cleverly analyse his situation, means, and the condition he is in and can make the most out of these and use whatever means he has at hand to the best advantage. Before he undertakes any task, he takes every possible precaution, foreseeing any future problems, and acts accordingly.

Everything he says is appropriate, his manner entirely composed, and his thoughts are the product of a clear mind and understanding.

If people of wisdom possess these qualities, it is because they live out their lives trying to earn Allah's approval and sincerely aiming for the Hereafter. The Qur'an reminds us that the Prophets sincerely turned towards the Hereafter and in accordance with the high morals they displayed they were people of strength and discernment.

And remember Our servants Ibrahim, Ishaq and Ya'qub, men of true strength and vision. We purified their sincerity through sincere remembrance of the Hereafter. They shall dwell with Us among the righteous whom we have chosen. (Surah Sad: 45-47)

WISDOM, DECISIVE SPEECH, AND THE ART OF PUBLIC SPEAKING

Another aspect of wisdom which most people fail to recognize is its ability to add purpose to one's mannerisms and speech. Most people miss the point that the actual source of such mannerisms and speech is wisdom. On the contrary, they think that wisdom is a quality that can be acquired through education and experience. That is why it is generally thought that the only way to speak well and persuasively is to memorize rules of influential speech by taking classes or reading books on how to speak effectively. These books outline when people should start and stop speaking, when they should laugh, and details such as these which are supposed to produce effective oratory. They believe that people can be successful speakers in relation to how well they follow these rules.

However, it is definitely not possible to bind effective speaking to any rules. On the contrary, truly effective speaking is not linked to any rules and is not memorized, rather it is a "sincere speech", which comes from the heart, without any difficulties, and without artificiality. And only people of wisdom possess this type of perfection in speech. The one who speaks with wisdom leaves a deep impression on the hearts of his listeners with the sincerity of his words.

One who is far from religion can make a good speech on a topic within his area of expertise with proper emphasis and by following the rules of speech. However, we shouldn't forget that the qualities mentioned do not reflect any wisdom in this speech. For a speech have wisdom, it has to be sincere and leave a deep impression on the hearts of the listeners. A wise person is someone who can explain what he wants in the most genuine and sincere way, with the most striking examples. In one verse, Allah points out the importance of wisdom by stating that He has given this quality to the Prophet Dawud (as):

We made his kingdom strong and gave him wisdom and decisive speech. (Surah Sad: 20)

As is seen in the verse, along with giving wisdom as a virtue, "decisive speech" is also mentioned. To attain such a blessing one doesn't need to have any special talent or expend any extraordinary effort. It is given by Allah to those who have faith and are sincere.

However, wisdom is not something that manifests itself only in speech. It is evinced also in a wise person's mannerisms and decisions, and in the analyses he makes. It is declared in the Qur'an that this important superior quality is given to many of the Prophets:

They are the ones to whom We gave the Book, Judgement and Prophethood... (Surat al-An'am: 89)

And with Allah's permission they routed them. Dawud killed Talut and Allah gave him kingship and wisdom and taught him whatever He willed... (Surat al-Baqara: 251)

"Yahya, take hold of the Book with vigour." We gave him judgement while still a child. (Surah Maryam: 12)

In other verses of the Quran, it is stated that Allah can give wisdom and insight to whomever He wills:

He gives wisdom to whomever He wills and he who has been given wisdom has been given great good. But no one pays heed but people of understanding. (Surat al-Baqara: 269)

From all these verses we can understand that this great blessing, given to a responsive person, brings about "strength of expression" and with it the "ability to persuade". A believer takes the opportunity to explain the true religion and morals of the Qur'an in the best possible way, with the qualities of wisdom, decisive speech, and apt expression, as Allah advises: **"Call to the way of your Lord with wisdom and fair admonition, and argue with them in the kindest way..."** (Surat an-Nahl: 125)

A SUPERIOR ANALYSIS ABILITY

Another important quality wisdom brings with it is the ability to "analyse things". Anyone can recognize and make comments on any given thing. However, of where people of wisdom excel is in their recognition always being appropriate and their ability to see details which others cannot. The secret of this appropriateness and fine recognition ability is that believers use the Qur'an as their guide and use their wisdom toward its ends. The Qur'an is Allah's just book. As a consequence, people who obey the Qur'an will definitely tread the most righteous path.

This ability of wise people makes for superiority and ease in every part of their lives. Above all else, they can analyse in detail the character of the people they meet. As a result they can easily determine their friends and enemies. By taking the characters Allah introduces in the Qur'an as their guide, they can understand others' characters in a very short period. Moreover, their ability to realize at the outset which events are in their favour and take precautions accordingly is a great advantage to them. Also, it is those with wisdom who can appreciate the beauties of the people around them, the details of which generally go unappreciated and the signs of wisdom they demonstrate.

Another important quality of wise people that merit attention, is that they do not need to make lengthy observations or gather detailed information before making correct assumptions. A wise person's chief quality is his ability to arrive at correct conclusions with as little evidence as is needed and in the briefest possible time.

A wise person can determine whether a person is lying by his mannerisms at that time, by inconsistencies in his speech, by his efforts to explain the situation in detail, by his restless behaviour, and many other factors depending on the situation. A person lacking wisdom will fully trust a person who is lying and even talk about his honesty. Because of this, he can go into a partnership with the dishonest person and suffer materially and spiritually as a consequence.

The reason why people lacking wisdom draw wrong conclusions and make wrong decisions under the same circumstances is that they don't follow the Qur'an's teachings. Allah therefore draws attention to the fact that only the wise can see and comprehend the examples given in the Qur'an and reminds us that people who know and who don't know are not the same:

Such metaphors—We devise them for mankind; but only those with knowledge understand them. (Surat al-'Ankabut: 43)

What of him who spends the night hours in prayer, prostrating himself and standing up, mindful of the Hereafter, hoping for the mercy of his Lord? Say: "Are they the same—those who know and those who do not know?" It is only people of understanding who pay heed. (Surat az-Zumar: 9)

ATTENTION AND CLEAR CONSCIENCE

In the Qur'an, Allah reminds people to heed Him and draws their attention to various topics:

Everything in the heavens and on the earth belongs to Allah. He knows what you are engaged upon. On the Day when they are returned to Him, He will inform them of what they did. Allah has knowledge of all things. (Surat an-Nur: 64)

What! Are they in doubt about the meeting with their Lord? What! Does He not encompass all things? (Surah Fussilat: 54)

Have they looked at the sky above them: how We structured it and made it beautiful and how there are no fissures in it? And the earth: how We stretched it out and cast firmly embedded mountains onto it and caused

luxuriant plants of every kind to grow in it, thus offer-
ing an insight and a reminder unto every human being
who turns to Allah. (Surah Qaf: 6-8)

As the above verses recall, Allah advises people to apply
their minds to thinking clearly, analyzing situations rightly, and
thus seeing realities. However, it shouldn't be forgotten that the
ability to focus our attention as mentioned in the Qur'an is a
quality evinced only by people of wisdom. We are told in the
Qur'an that only the wise reflect on and take the advice of the
teachings of the Qur'an:

... But only people of understanding pay heed. (Surah
Al 'Imran: 7)

It is a Book We have sent down to you, full of blessing,
so let people of understanding ponder upon its Signs
and take heed. (Surah Sad: 29)

So, people of wisdom who focus their attention as the Qur'an
instructs can see the whole of reality. They grasp primarily that
there is no god other than Allah, that He is the owner of the
whole universe, and that the Hereafter is a definite reality.

As we dwelt upon previously, a clear conscience and close attention manifest themselves at all times in a wise person's life.
Knowing that Allah created everything for a reason, that everything they experience and every utterance they hear are parts of
the test created for them, and that they're responsible for all the
things they're faced with, sharpens their attention. As a result,
they can sense a developing threat in their environment and
take the appropriate measures before anyone else. In the same
way, they can instantly determine a positive development by
paying close attention.

It is true that intelligence also provides people with a certain superior awareness. But the difference made by wisdom in this case is that it notices details that intelligence can't distinguish and this gives the opportunity to analyse, take precautions, and make timely decisions. For example, an intelligent and alert person will realize that there is a burglar in his house by paying attention to the sounds coming from the basement. A wise person, on the other hand, is one who will take definite precautions and bring lasting solutions to the possibility of a burglary before the situation develops to this extent. He will have thought about all the alternatives to the possibility of a burglar entering and worked extensively on this issue. For example, he will set up a sophisticated security system that will definitely prevent a stranger from entering the house.

So, this is the ideal type of attention one should be capable of. A wise person does not just cope with a dangerous situation as it's happening. He takes precautions before the danger begins to develop, before he faces such a situation, even where many of the relevant factors are not immediately obvious. After he has determined these actual dangers, he takes definite precautions in order not to be subjected to them.

A STRONG PERSONALITY

A wise person knows that all creatures alive or not, submit to Allah and nothing ever happens in this universe without His permission. His submission to and the trust he reposes in Allah enable him to be fearless of anyone or anything except Allah and thus enables him to develop a strong personality. Because he knows that Allah controls everything, his behaviour towards others or in different situations does not change. As he strives to earn Allah's approval and not that of other people, he doesn't ever make a concession in his personality, behaviour, and morals for any personal benefit.

However, we should remember that the true meaning of a "strong personality" is actually different from the way it is used in ignorant circles. People far from religion, believe that the only way to build up the personality is through arrogance, formality, and gravity. They think that the more a person makes his difference from and superiority over others felt by those around him, the greater the personality he has. However, this kind of conduct does not denote a strong inner personality but is rather aimed at hoodwinking others and projecting "an image" of an individual with a great personality to those around him.

Real personality has nothing to do with pride, gravity, formality, or outward appearances. According to the Qur'an, a strong personality indicates one's fear of Allah and as a result of this, shows determination in living by the morals of the Qur'an. One with strength of personality never compromises upon the truths told to him by Allah for any reason or for any worldly gain, and never condescends to crude or unpleasant behaviour. So, these are the qualities that give a person a real personality and people who are steadfast in maintaining these qualities are people of wisdom. People of wisdom who never stray from the right path are given this good news in the Qur'an:

The angels descend on those who say, "Our Lord is Allah", and then take the right path to Him. They say: "Do not fear and do not grieve but rejoice in the Garden [i.e., Paradise] you have been promised." (Surah Fussilat: 30)

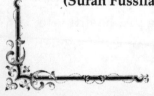

ALLAH'S HELP AND SUPPORT

You who believe! You are only responsible for yourselves. The misguided cannot harm you as long as you
are guided. All of you will return to Allah and He will
inform you about what you were doing. (Surat al-
Ma'ida: 105)

In this verse Allah informs the believers of a very important
reality: unbelievers cannot misguide believers.

The right path can be reached only by those who have faith
and who follow the teachings of the Qur'an. Because such people always take the teachings of the Qur'an as their guide and
live their lives accordingly, they always receive Allah's help and
support in return. Allah helps believers and has promised to
help those who help his religion:

... Allah will certainly help those who help Him—
Allah is Powerful, Almighty. (Surat al-Hajj: 40)

Allah explains in another verse, that He helps and supports
those that believe in Him sincerely and that He makes things
easier for them:

As for him who gives [generously], performs his duty
and acts charitably in the finest manner, We shall facili-
tate an easy way for him. (Surat al-Layl: 5-7)
... Whoever heeds Allah—He will make matters easy for
him. (Surat al-Talaq: 4)
Those who seek the protection of Allah, His Messenger
and the faithful must know that it is Allah's followers
who are victorious! (Surat al-Ma'ida: 56)

In Surat al-Anbiya', Allah points out that the truth and justness always wins over falsehood. This is why, people of wisdom
who follow the right path always win against those who hide

behind falsehood. Allah tells us this truth:

We hurl the truth against falsehood and it cuts right through it and it vanishes clean away!... (Surat al-Anbiya': 18)

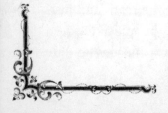

EXAMPLES OF WISDOM IN EVERYDAY LIFE

From the beginning of the book we have mentioned how wisdom can be acquired and improved. However, the important thing is for people to learn how to apply wisdom in their lives and find out where and when they can use it. Wisdom is not a quality that comes about with great inventions or something that enables success only in important areas of our lives. On the contrary, it is reflected in our daily lives, from cleaning to eating, from clothing to art. For this reason, we will give examples of how wisdom is applied to everyday life in this chapter.

THE THOUGHT PROCESSES OF A WISE PERSON

Above all else, the wise person thinks of how he can earn Allah's approval at all times. He analyses everything that goes on around him and, abiding by his conscience, decides what is the best thing for him to do in that situation.

He never restrains his thoughts, he thinks freely. His horizon is as broad as possible. He is freed of all bigotry, baseless fears and dogmas.

Because he doesn't place any limits on his thoughts, he always comes up with ideas which are straightforward but very effective.

He never occupies his mind with unnecessary thoughts. He never spends his time on things that will not benefit him, that will waste his time, or that will hinder him from spending time on truly important issues.

He puts the needs of the people around him first. He thinks of how he can help these people with their safety, health, and happiness and, if there are any obstacles in achieving these goals, he deals with them without any delay.

He always thinks of things that can be of benefit to religion and believers. He always wants and tries to do beneficial things.

A wise person also plans ahead of time. He focuses his thoughts on whatever he is aiming at. He never concentrates on trivial details.

He thinks of events in stages. He takes precautions by predicting what will happen a few stages later, what the potential dangers might be, or what improvements are likely to happen.

He also thinks of past events. He draws the most sensible and wise conclusions from his experiences and hence accumulates valuable lessons that he may apply in the future.

Whenever negative or wrong things come to mind, he knows that they are only Satan's deceitful words and he takes refuge in Allah.

And with the knowledge that there is a purpose and beauty in everything Allah has created, he thinks "there is good in all".

A WISE PERSON'S CONVERSATIONS AND SPEECH

A wise person's utterances are the most fitting, wise, genuine, and helpful. Because his vision is broad, the examples he gives are most original and therefore the most effective. Instead of talking excessively he prefers to talk briefly of worthwhile things. He talks when it is necessary and when it is most appropriate. In his wisdom, he determines when it is best to speak and when it is not. For example, he doesn't engage a person in a hurry with unimportant things.

Moreover, he doesn't waste his time by making pointless speeches on meaningless topics. And he only talks about an important topic in relation to its significance.

A wise person makes sincere speeches straight from the heart. He doesn't have a set type. He knows that a truly effective speech is one that comes from within.

Neither does he speak in a monotonous voice, or repeat the same words, sentences, and style. He doesn't use abusive or hurtful words in his speech. He never upsets others by mocking them. He always conveys what he wants to in a clear and precise way.

A WISE PERSON'S UNDERSTANDING OF ART AND DECORATION

A wise person takes Allah's artistry as an example above all else. He knows that the imagery of Heaven mentioned in the Qur'an draws attention to materials that give the most pleasure to the human soul and so he tries to imitate these decorations in worldly terms.

As with everything else, he doesn't constrain himself with any rules on this issue. He knows that he doesn't have to place constraints on his style by following fashion. He can make use of all the civilizations and cultures throughout history and be inspired by all the works of art they left behind.

Among these works of art he can analyse which ones are the most appealing to the human eye and give pleasure to the human soul in terms of art and aesthetics. And by combining the most aesthetic pieces, he can come up with an incomparable masterpiece.

Such a person can also combine comfort with art and aesthetics. For this reason, it is very pleasurable as well as comfortable to live in a place which a wise person has decorated. The pieces he chooses are designed to be the most hygienic for human health, most comfortable, easiest to clean, and the most hardwearing, as well as being aesthetically pleasing. For example, he won't use a piece for its good appearance, if it contains harmful smells or chemicals. Instead, he can achieve the same beauty by using different materials.

In addition, he can continuously make new changes in decoration. With the same materials, in the same setting he can put together hundreds of totally different kinds of decor. He never allows for the decoration of the place he is living in to become monotonous. He always makes the place he lives in beautiful by making small or big changes.

Decoration put together by the power of wisdom won't include anything unappealing to the eye. The light and sound arrangement, and the choice of colours would be the most calming and pleasurable to the human eye and soul.

He gives importance to symmetry in decoration. He can calculate the pleasure of symmetry and confusion of asymmetry that the human eye and soul will experience.

THE DEXTERITY OF A WISE PERSON

A wise person achieves dexterity by using his wisdom. When he faces a situation that requires him to use skill, he appraises the available options in the best way, plans which task performed in which way will yield the best result, and when he applies this, he achieves the perfect solution. He carries out every job in the most practical way. When he faces a sudden problem,

Examples of Wisdom in Everyday Life

47

he deals with it in the best way with whatever he has to hand, if it is insufficient.

When he faces a setback, he firstly figures out if he can offset it by whatever means and knowledge he possesses. If he can solve the problem he tries to get rid of it. But if the problem is a technical one and surpasses his ability, he solves the problem by calling on the most competent and knowledgeable person in the field, without wasting any time.

He brings lasting and clear solutions to problems, not temporary or primitive ones. He knows that the harm that may be done if the task is not correctly carried out will require greater effort to reverse than that initially expended on the problem.

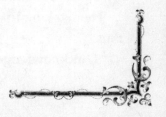

EXAMPLES OF WISDOM
IN THE QUR'AN

People with wisdom are reminded to take warning by reflecting on the anecdotes in the Qur'an. In Surah Yusuf it is commanded as:

> There is instruction in their stories for people of understanding. This is no invented talk but a confirmation of previous scripture, a clarification of everything, and a guide and a mercy for all those who believe. (Surah Yusuf: 111)

With the above verse in mind, we will draw attention to a few instances of the insightful behaviour cited in the stories of the Prophets in the Qur'an which portray the superiority achieved by wisdom.

THE UNSURPASSABLE BARRIER CONSTRUCTED BY DHU'L-QARNAYN (AS)

The Qur'an tells the Prophet Dhu'l-Qarnayn (as), to whom Allah gave much power and knowledge. The Qur'an begins his story thus:

> They will ask you about Dhu'l-Qarnayn. Say: "I will tell you something about him". We gave him power and authority on the earth and granted him the means to achieve all things. (Surat al-Kahf: 83-84)

Then, taking up the main part of the narrative, it continues thus:

> Our knowledge encompasses all that happened to him.

> Then he followed a path until he arrived between the
> Two Mountains where he found a people scarcely able
> to understand a word. They said, "Dhu'l-Qarnayn!
> Yajuj (Gog) and Majuj (Magog) are ravaging the land.
> Can we, therefore, pay tribute to you in return for your
> constructing a barrier between us and them?" He said,
> "The power my Lord has granted me is better than any
> tribute. Just give me a strong helping hand and I will
> build a solid barrier between you and them." (Surat al-
> Kahf: 91-95)

As is seen in the verse, Dhu'l-Qarnayn (as) responds to the re-
quests of the local people. Then, Dhu'l-Qarnayn (as) builds the
barrier in such a clever way, to protect the people from Yajuj and
Majuj, that it has never been climbed over or breached:

> "Bring me ingots of iron!" he said. Then, when he had
> made it level between the two high mountain-sides, he
> said, "Ply your bellows!" and when the iron blocks be-
> came red-hot, he said, "Bring me molten brass to pour
> over them". Yajuj and Majuj, therefore, were unable to
> climb over it, nor were they able to make a breach in it.
> (Surat al-Kahf: 96-97)

Dhu'l-Qarnayn (as)'s success is without a doubt the result of
his superior wisdom. To be able to create a barrier that cannot be
climbed over, he chooses to use the strongest material in the
most effective way possible. First, he puts in position the masses
of iron and then applies heat to them until they become red-hot.
But, very strong as the barrier now is, he doesn't leave it like this.
To make it foolproof, he pours molten brass over it. Thus, he
makes the barrier strong enough to be quite unscalable and also
impenetrable.

The wisdom Dhu'l-Qarnayn (as) shows in building this barrier is a good example of how faith strengthens the mind. The most striking quality of people with wisdom is the fact that they don't resort to temporary or weak solutions, but rather make the most of what they have and devise the best precautions. That is to say, they get rid of the danger so that its threat is reduced to the extent of not even hurting a single person. This wisdom is clearly visible in the barrier Dhu'l-Qarnayn (as) constructed.

THE PROPHET IBRAHIM (AS)'S STRATEGY AGAINST THE IDOLS

The Qur'an states the numerous instances of the Prophet Ibrahim (as)'s wisdom. One of these is the plan he devised to warn his people who worshipped idols and show them the right path. To prove to his people that the idols they worshipped were merely pieces of stone and of no use to anyone, he first had to distance them from where the idols were situated. Thanks to his foresight, he successfully accomplished what he wanted to. He simply told them that he was sick, and they all fled the area in fear of catching his sickness:

> He lifted up his eyes to the stars and said, "I am sick!" So his people turned their backs on him and went off. He turned surreptitiously to their idols and said, "Will you not eat your offerings? What is the matter with you that you do not speak?" With that, he turned on them, striking them down with his right hand. (Surat as-Saffat: 88-93)
> He broke them all in pieces, except for the biggest one, so that they would have it to consult! (Surat al-Anbiya': 58)

When his people scattered from the area, the Prophet Ibrahim (as) went to where the idols were and shattered them into pieces, except the largest one. Without a doubt there is a great reason why he left the biggest idol intact. The reason for this would be revealed when his people returned. On their return, his people were shocked with what had happened to the stones they worshipped and started questioning who might have done this:

Some asked: "Who has done this to our gods? He is definitely one of the wrongdoers!" Others replied: "We heard a young man mentioning them. They call him Ibrahim". They said, "Bring him here before the people's eyes so that they can be witnesses". (Surat al-Anbiya': 59-61)

When they asked the Prophet Ibrahim (as) what had happened, he pointed to the biggest idol and told them to ask him. When they realized that the stone could not talk and explain what had happened there, they had to admit that these stones did not have any power:

They asked, "Did you do this to our gods, Ibrahim?" He replied, "No, this one, the biggest of them, did it. Ask them if they are able to speak!" So they returned to [blaming] themselves and said [to each other], "Indeed you are the wrongdoers". But then they relapsed back into their disbelief: "You know full well these idols cannot talk". (Surat al-Anbiya': 62-65)

In reply to this conversation the Prophet Ibrahim (as) said:

"Do you then worship, instead of Allah, what cannot help or harm you in any way?" (Surat al-Anbiya': 66)
"Do you worship something you have carved with your own hands, when it was Allah Who created both you

and all that you have made?" (Surat as-Saffat: 95-96)

As a result of the Prophet proving to them that these idols they worshipped were of no avail to anyone, they saw as a matter of conscience that what they had done was irrational, even though it was for a brief moment. The Prophet Ibrahim (as) had shown them the truth with his wisdom and got them to confess their wrongdoings. Even so they insisted on worshipping idols after this incident.

THE OBVIOUS WISDOM IN THE WORDS OF THE PROPHET IBRAHIM (AS)

Another example given in the Qur'an of the Prophet Ibrahim (as)'s wisdom is conveyed in the conversation that takes place between him and a person whom Allah has made rich and powerful. With the clear mind the Prophet Ibrahim (as) earned by obeying religion, he was able to win an argument against a person who, far from religion, argued with him about Allah with his crooked reasoning. The conversation between the Prophet Ibrahim (as) and the person who was given sovereignty is as follows:

Have you not heard of him, who argued with Ibrahim about his Lord, because Allah had given him sovereignty? Ibrahim said, "My Lord is He Who gives life and causes to death". He said, "I too give life and cause death". Ibrahim said, "Allah makes the sun come from the East. Make it come from the West". The unbeliever was dumbfounded. Allah does not guide evil-doers. (Surat al-Baqara: 258)

The Prophet Ibrahim (as) gives a very sound answer to this unbeliever who says he too can "give life and cause death". In the light of this answer, he is dumbfounded in the face of wisdom and truth.

THE PROPHET MUHAMMAD (SAAS)'S EARLY DEPARTURE FROM HIS HOUSE

Allah draws attention to yet another perceptive action mentioned in the Qur'an, **"Remember when you left your family early in the day to install the believers in their battle stations. Allah is All-Hearing, All-Knowing"**. (Surah Al 'Imran: 121) The Prophet Muhammad (saas) had left his house early on the brink of battle to guarantee the safety and success of the believers. Without a doubt, this approach of his is an important example of the power of wisdom for all believers.

As can be understood from this example, one of the wisest precautions to take is to act early in times of great duress. This is because one who acts in advance can organize everything which needs to be done beforehand, and also gets the opportunity to find out what is needed, and which details may have been overlooked. Hence, the panic and excitement that may be caused by doing something at the last minute in a rush will be prevented. Just knowing that there is enough time allows people to think calmly and clearly. Also in a situation where it is important to act in a group, it is possible to exchange ideas to get a consensus in the given time frame.

Furthermore, acting ahead of time gives a person an important advantage in the face of unanticipated and unwanted events. When acting in advance, it is possible to compensate for any problem that arises.

Our Prophet Muhammad (saas) proves his superior wisdom by planning ahead and showing us the advantages of acting early. By going to the battlefield early, he designates everyone's duty and places each one at the most strategic spot.

THE PROPHET YA'QUB (AS)'S KEEPING AN IMPORTANT ISSUE A SECRET FROM PEOPLE WITH BAD INTENTIONS

In the previous chapters we drew attention to one of the most important qualities of a person with wisdom, i.e. that they calculate where every step they take may lead them. Indeed, with his sagacity and discernment, a person with wisdom never neglects to look at his past experiences and the knowledge he has accumulated before he starts something new. In the same way, he bears in mind the details of all the likely possible contingencies. In so acting he can take the wisest of precautions.

One of the Prophets mentioned in the Qur'an who was so wise in conduct is the Prophet Ya'qub (as). The Prophet Ya'qub (as) realized that his love for his son Yusuf (as) was sparking jealousy among his other sons and feared that they might do something harmful to Yusuf (as). Allah heralds in His verses the fact that Ya'qub (as) was right in being anxious. In Surah Yusuf, we are told to us what Yusuf (as)'s brothers thought of him:

> **They declared, "Why! Yusuf and his brother are dearer to our father than we are, although we constitute a powerful group. Our father is clearly making a mistake". (Surah Yusuf: 8)**

When Yusuf (as) tells Ya'qub (as) of his dream in which the stars, the sun, and the moon bow down to him, Ya'qub (as) realizes that this dream may point to the fact that Yusuf (as) is a special person chosen by Allah. Because Ya'qub (as) is aware of what Yusuf (as)'s brothers think of him, he tells Yusuf (as) not to mention his dream to his brothers, since this information may fuel the other siblings' jealousy even more and cause them to harm Yusuf (as).

This conversation between Ya'qub (as) and Yusuf (as) is narrated in the Qur'an as follows:

> **When Yusuf told his father, "Father! I saw eleven bright stars, and the sun and moon as well. I saw them all prostrate in front of me". He said, "My son, don't tell your brothers your dream lest they devise some scheme to injure you, Satan is a clear-cut enemy to man. Accordingly, your Lord will pick you out and teach you the true meaning of events and perfectly fulfil His blessing on you as well as on the family of Ya'qub, as He fulfiled it perfectly before upon your forebears, Ibrahim and Ishaq. Most certainly your Lord is All-Knowing, and Wise". (Surah Yusuf: 4-6)**

As is clear, Ya'qub (as) thinks of the possible outcome of jealousy and takes precautions accordingly. As Allah tell us **"In Yusuf and his brothers there are Signs for every one of those who wants to ask."** (Surah Yusuf: 7), believers should take heed of the signs of wisdom found in Yusuf (as)'s story. And to achieve such wisdom themselves, they should make efforts to increase their closeness to Allah and live by the teachings of the Qur'an.

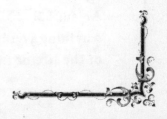

HOW IS THOUGHTLESSNESS DEFINED IN THE QUR'AN?

As we have been explaining since the beginning of this book, wisdom is earned by a person abiding entirely by his conscience, choosing to live his life in a way that pleases Allah and is in accordance with the Qur'an, and as a result reaching perfection of thought and conduct. Also, it is comprehending the reason for his being and Allah's infinite power.

People who are not aware of these things are thoughtless. Most people never imagine that the personalities they see on television, their neighbours, university graduates, or successful businessmen can be thoughtless. However, being thoughtless means leading a life of ignorance, and because of this leading a miserable and difficult life, when they can live a life by the teachings of the Qur'an, which guides people to the best way of living both in this world and the Hereafter. So it is possible for a person to meet many thoughtless people around him.

In the Qur'an, Allah draws attention to the mistake people make with regard to worldly life and ignorance, and calls upon them to reflect on this and learn from it:

> The life of the world is nothing but a game and a diversion. The Hereafter is better for those who guard against evil. So will you not use your reason? (Surat al-An'am: 32)
>
> Anything you have been given is only the enjoyment of the life of this world and its finery. What is with

Allah's reward is better and longer lasting. So will you
not use your reason? (Surat al-Qasas: 60)
We have sent down to you a Book containing your ad-
monishment. So will you not use your reason? (Surat
al-Anbiya': 10)
... Have they not travelled in the land and seen the final
fate of those before them? The abode of the Hereafter is
better for those who guard against evil. So will you not
use your reason? (Surah Yusuf: 109)

Even after the reminders in the Qur'an, such individuals as
do not wish to comprehend the reality of this world and the
Hereafter are those who do not use their reason, as the Qur'an
mentions. Allah tells us of how these people figure in His eyes:

The worst of beasts in Allah's sight are the deaf and
dumb who do not use their reason. (Surat al-Anfal: 22)

What is of true importance is that such people do not have the
ability to differentiate between wisdom and thoughtlessness;
they cannot see the situation they are in. So they think that wise
people are thoughtless, and thoughtless people like themselves
are wise. Because they do not fear Allah or concede the slightest
possibility of having to account for the things they have done in
this world, they assume that the path they are following is the
right one. The Qur'an gives an example of their false mentality:

When they are told, "Believe in the way that others believe", they say, "What! Are we to believe in the way
that fools believe?" No indeed! They are the fools, but
they do not know it. (Surat al-Baqara: 13)

As clarified in the above verse, a thoughtless person thinking
he is wise and not admitting any possibility of being in the
wrong is the result of being thoughtless. Such people as do not

possess any real perception are defined as blind and deaf in the Qur'an, even though they have no physical deficiencies. It is because these people cannot properly comprehend reality in general, nor can they grasp the realities they see and hear. For example, they cannot see Allah's greatness by looking at the perfect creation in the universe. Even if they do see it, they pretend not to have seen it, as they are thoughtless and do not listen to the voice of their conscience. Or they do not hear those who call them to the right path and explain to them the teachings of the Qur'an. Actually, they do hear them physically, but they go on living their lives heedlessly as if they had never listened to them. The situation they are in is explained in the Qur'an as:

> Among them there are some who listen to you. But can you make the deaf hear incapable as they are of understanding? Among them there are some who look at you. But can you guide the blind, bereft as they are of sight? Allah does not wrong people in any way; rather it is people who wrong themselves. On the day We gather them together—when it will seem as if they had tarried no more than an hour of a single day—they will recognize one another. Those who denied the meeting with Allah and did not follow the right path will be lost. (Surah Yunus: 42-45)

As can be understood from all these explanations in the Qur'an, by detaching people from their humanness, a lack of wisdom makes people unable to comprehend and see and hear realities. This is explained in other verses:

> We created many of the jinn and mankind for Hell. They have hearts they do not understand with. They have eyes they do not see with. They have ears they do

not hear with. Such people are like cattle. No, they are
even further astray! They are the unaware. (Surat al-
A'raf: 179)

The unbelievers are like beasts, which, call out to them
as one may cannot hear anything but a cry and a call.
Deaf, dumb and blind, they understand nothing. (Surat
al-Baqara: 171)

The reason why in the following pages we will be mentioning
things that fog the mind is to warn people against the dangers of
a lack of understanding. Because one who fails to rid himself of
wrongful things that block his mind will experience great losses
in this world and the Hereafter. Allah points out that those who
lack understanding will remember their worldly life in the
Hereafter with regret and say:

If only we had really listened and understood, we
would not now have been the heirs of Hell. (Surat al-
Mulk: 10)

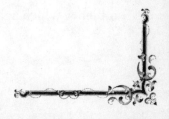

OBSTACLES TO WISDOM

As we mentioned in the earlier chapters, everyone has the opportunity to be wise and make use of the good things wisdom provides. To achieve this, he has to see the greatness of Allah and live his life in this world as His proper servant. One who comprehends this is following the most righteous path. Because the only guide that truly guides and shows the believer the right way is the Qur'an. Allah reveals all the things that block the mind and ways to overcome these in the Qur'an.

The mind of someone who obeys Allah's call is freed of all the filthy things that clog it up and it becomes clean and clear. The thing that provides this clarity of mind is the clear logic and ability to think righteously achieved by the Qur'an and having faith. A person's understanding develops more and more as he becomes purified of ignorant people's skewed logic and way of thinking, and the filth this type of life brings, and instead lives by the morals of the Qur'an. As he becomes freed of all ill-mannered habits, he also becomes freed of the restraints on his mind, and so becomes one of the people of wisdom mentioned in the Qur'an. Failing this, his mind will be filled with obstacles and he will knowingly lead himself to ruin.

In this section we will dwell on obstructions to wisdom mentioned in the Qur'an. Also, we will present the solutions to these problems, which again are covered only in the Qur'an.

SHIRK - ATTRIBUTING PARTNERS TO ALLAH

Shirk means attributing partners to Allah and worshipping gods other than Allah. The values a person, who commits *shirk*, deifies can be making his ideals and passions the purpose of his life, as well as deifying a person or another living thing. If he sees these values as more important than pleasing Allah and if he feels the same or more love towards them, it means he is associating them with Allah.

This is the *shirk* that is explained in the Qur'an, but most people are unaware of this real meaning of *shirk*. They link "associating other gods with Allah" with people who worshipped the idols they carved at the time of the Prophet Muhammad (saas). However, in our times thousands of different types of *shirk* can occur. For a person to say he believes in Allah while at the same time not living his life in order to please Him, not practicing the rituals He prescribed, not living by the morals Allah approves of, but instead spending his time trying to turn his worldly ideals into realities is also a form of *shirk*. In the same way, forgetting our Creator and Provider, preferring and valuing another being above Him, and, instead of pleasing Allah, using his intellect and spending his time on trying to make this other being happy and love him is also a *shirk*. It is possible to run into people who associate their spouses, children, mothers, fathers, marriage, school, career, possessions, worldly ambitions, and even themselves with Allah. These people fall into the error of *shirk* by in a way deifying these concepts or people of whom they think so highly, and orienting all their deeds according to this viewpoint. However, there is no god other than Allah, and to say the opposite would be a lie against Allah and be unappreciative of Allah's greatness.

One who cannot appreciate the power of Allah, Who faultlessly created him and the whole of the universe, is without a doubt in a state of thoughtlessness. Because a person, who associates other gods with Allah, cannot live a happy life in this world and will have to face Allah's punishment in the Hereafter. Allah tells us in the Qur'an that the actions of those who associate partners with Allah will result in nothing:

> **It has been revealed to you and those before you: "If you associate others with Allah, your actions will come to nothing and you will be among the losers". (Surat az-Zumar: 65)**

It is also explained that people who commit *shirk* will not be forgiven:

> **Allah does not forgive anything being associated with Him, but He forgives whoever He wills for anything other than that. Anyone who associates something with Allah has committed a terrible crime. (Surat an-Nisa': 48)**

In another verse, the Prophet Luqman (as) gives his son advice by reminding him that *shirk* is a terrible wrong:

> **Luqman said to his son, counselling him, "My son, do not associate anything with Allah. Associating others with Him is a terrible wrong". (Surah Luqman: 13)**

As can be seen in the verse, Allah describes *shirk* as a wrong. *Shirk*, as well as committing an offence against Allah, is wronging one's self. Since a person who commits *shirk* has also fallen into a great error, his life that he has based on faulty thinking is also full of mistakes. In this situation, it is not possible to mention wisdom or the benefits it gives to a person who associates partners with Allah. Because, Allah seals the hearts and blocks the ability to comprehend of those who deny Him and invent a lie against Him, becoming unjustifiably arrogant.

To be saved from such a situation and become a person who can really think, the individual has to be able to comprehend the greatness of Allah and not worship anything other than Allah. This is the only way the veil can be lifted from his wisdom and his mind can be cleared.

HEEDLESSNESS

Heedlessness means that a person cannot see, sense, or be aware of the realities around him. As mentioned in the Qur'an, a heedless person's most noticeable trait is his inability to comprehend the numerous proofs of creation, the reason for his being, the closeness of death, the reality of the Hereafter, and similar topics that are vital for him. In one verse of the Qur'an, Allah indicates the situation of heedless people:

Mankind's Reckoning has drawn very close to them, yet they heedlessly turn away. (Surat al-Anbiya': 1)

As mentioned in the verse above, one who lives his life heedlessly acts as if he is unaware of the fast approaching Day of Judgement and as if he will never be accountable for the things he has done. Because, heedlessness is like a state of slumber, which veils the mind, prevents perceptive behaviour and nullifies appropriate decision-making skills. One who is in this state all his life, becomes distant from the truth and because he cannot use his mind, he becomes unable to differentiate right from wrong, and puts himself in situations that will be harmful to him both in this world and the Hereafter.

The cause of heedlessness is a person's remoteness from Allah and his Book, and the failure to live a life of faith. The following is an example Allah gives to describe the situation these people are in:

We created many of the jinn and mankind for Hell. They have hearts they do not understand with. They have eyes they do not see with. They have ears they do not hear with. Such people are like cattle. No, they are even further astray! They are the unaware. (Surat al-A'raf: 179)

The situation such people are in is clearly explained in the Qur'an, but they are not even aware of this reality either. Since one who is oblivious would never see himself as being "oblivious", he would not even admit that there could be any such possibility.

A wise person on the contrary can recognize the state these heedless people are in at first glance. This is because people of wisdom approach events by using the Qur'an as their guide. The Qur'an informs us of the behaviour, the mentality, and the reasoning a heedless person displays. For this reason, a heedless person gives himself away at every turn. As long as this person is in this state of mind, he will manifest his state by his actions and thoughts, even if he has had a good education and is a perfect speaker.

Foremost among the signs that shows a person's heedless state is his judging everything by its outward appearances. The person in question thinks that everything consists of the things he sees. And because of this, he evaluates things wrongly and reaches wrong conclusions. He mostly cannot see the benefits and reasons behind events.

Another major mistake heedlessness brings about is for people to forget the reason for their creation and existence in this world. Such people become blind to the proofs of the existence of Allah Who has created them, and fall into a state of denial without thinking of what they will face in the Hereafter as a result of their actions in this world. This is because these heedless people cannot see the reality and intolerableness of Hellfire with a clear consciousness and do not, by reflecting upon it, fear it. Those who pretend not to understand their mistake in this world, will deeply regret Hell when they are face to face with it. That day the cover of heedlessness will be lifted and they will be given the power to evaluate everything they did throughout their lives with a clear consciousness. But, they will not have the chance to compensate for their heedlessness, which they did not try to correct even though they had been warned to do so many times. It is stated in the verse:

When the True Promise is very close, the eyes of those who have disbelieved will be transfixed and they will cry out: "Alas for us! We were unmindful of this! No, rather we were definitely wrongdoers". (Surat al-Anbiya': 97)

In Surah Qaf, the situation these people, who did not appreciate the numerous blessings Allah gave them and preferred blindness in the world, will face in the Hereafter is explained as:

The Trumpet will be blown. That is the Day of the Threat. Every self will come attended by one who will drive it on and by a witness: One will say "You were heedless of this so We have stripped you of your veil and today your sight is sharp". His inseparable comrade will say, "My testimony is ready to hand". Then a voice will cry: "Hurl into Hell every obdurate unbeliever". (Surah Qaf: 20-24)

As we can see in the verses above, it is great thoughtlessness for a person to knowingly lead his life in a state that results in destruction. The damage to the mind of one who has turned away from the truth, despite the advice he has been given, will negatively affect his life in this world and the Hereafter. It is for this reason that Allah warns people against such dangers and reminds them not to be seized by heedlessness:

> Remember your Lord deep in your soul humbly and fearfully, without ostentation, in the morning and in the evening. Do not be one of the unaware. (Surat al-A'raf: 205)

> Restrain yourself patiently with those who pray to their Lord morning and evening, seeking His pleasure. Do not turn your eyes from them, desiring the attractions of this world. And do not obey someone whose heart We have made neglectful of Our remembrance and who follows his own whims and desires and whose life has transgressed all bounds. (Surat al-Kahf: 28)

> Warn them of the Day of Bitter Regret when our decree shall be fulfiled. But they take no notice. They do not believe. (Surah Maryam: 39)

WORLDLY GREED

Allah has enhanced the world with many blessings that are pleasing to humankind. And has informed them that they can use these however they want to. But, along with this He has told them to be thankful for all these blessings and not to forget the Hereafter by being too preoccupied with greed in this world. This is because the life people lead in this world is not their real life. Their real life is the life of the Hereafter that starts with their death and continues till infinity. For this reason, forgetting the Hereafter and remaining engrossed with greed for 70-80 years of worldly life shows great heedlessness.

As a matter of fact, those who forget the Hereafter are deprived of the many beauties of this world and the blessings of the Hereafter. The effects of this deprivation in this world can be firstly seen in their understanding. People, who become passionately attached to this life, cannot properly assess the reason for their creation, their responsibilities towards Allah, and death and life after death, having become unable to think clearly. This situation shows that they are actually in a state of deception, while they think that they are doing the right things.

Because of their distorted value judgements, they think the real meaning of life consists of material things like money, wealth, and property, beauty, reputation, fame, respect, and leaving wealth and a respectable name for those they leave behind. And they spend all their lives trying to gain all these assets whereas, in fact, as our Prophet (as) has also advised, *"the best richness is the richness of the soul."* (Bukhari)

Yet, such people spend years trying to achieve a respectable position in the eyes of others and search for ways to gain their appreciation, but they do not think for a moment that they need to thank Allah, Who created them and given them life, Who presented them with countless blessings and continual sustenance, and helped them in all their affairs. Or, they spend their days working hard without stopping to rest so as to be richer than everybody else and are always in quest of new projects, but they do not think that it is Allah Who has given them their riches and fail to set aside the time to perform their duties as His servants.

So, as a result of the wrong choice they make, they are deprived of the most valuable blessing given to mankind in this world—the ability to reason. In this state of thoughtlessness, they turn to denial and because of this they lose Heaven and face Hell in the Hereafter. In the Qur'an, Allah explains the situation of **"'those who took their religion as a diversion and a game, and were deluded by the life of the world'. Today We will forget them just as they forgot the encounter of this Day and denied Our Signs."** (Surat al-A'raf: 51)

It is pointed out that unbelievers **"rejoice in the life of the world. Yet the life of the world, compared to the Hereafter, is only fleeting enjoyment."** (Surat ar-Ra'd: 26)

What people have to do to rid themselves of this thoughtlessness that leads them to destruction is very simple: if they realize that the blessings they are given in this world are all granted by Allah and if they do not forget that the real reason for their existence is to seek Allah's approval, they will not have any obstacles to block or pressure their minds. Allah's promise to His sincere servants is as follows:

> **To those who act rightly, male or female, being believers, We will give a good life and We will recompense them according to their noblest deeds. (Surat an-Nahl: 97)**

COMPLYING WITH SATAN

In one of his verses, Allah, by saying, **"You who believe! Enter absolutely into peace [Islam]. Do not follow in the footsteps of Satan. He is your outright enemy"** (Surat al-Baqara: 208) calls upon people to keep away from complying with Satan and following in his footsteps. Because, as is stated in the verse,

Satan is the enemy of human beings. He wants to divert people from the right path and in doing so cause them to face harm in this world and the next. One strategy he resorts to in achieving his aim is to occupy people's minds with groundless suspicions, and unfounded and illogical issues, so that he can prevent them from thinking straight and behaving rationally. Such attempts on the part of Satan are explained thus in the Qur'an:

> **[Satan said:] "I will lead them astray and fill them with false hopes..." (Surat an-Nisa': 119)**

Satan, in pursuit of his aim, continues to whisper "varnished falsehoods" to people till the end of their lives and tries to prevent them from using their reason. He strives to make them forget Allah's infinite power and to distance them from the Qur'an. But, it shouldn't be forgotten that Satan does not possess any strength of his own. Allah created him as He did all of creation. Satan also submitted to Allah; he cannot do anything without Allah's permission. Allah tells us that He reprieved Satan till Judgement Day to test people, see which ones would comply with him and turn away from the truth and which ones would show loyalty to Allah by not being fooled by Satan's ploys:

> **He [Satan] said: "My Lord, grant me a reprieve until the Day of Resurrection". He [Allah] said: "You are among the reprieved until the Appointed Day". Satan replied: "I swear by your might, that I will mislead all of them except for Your chosen servants". (Surah Sad: 79-83)**

At the same time Allah in His verse: **"... Satan's scheming is always feeble"** (Surat an-Nisa': 76) draws attention to the fact that Satan's traps and his innuendoes are based on extremely unsound logic. Also, according to the previous verse, He informs us that Satan has no effect on sincere believers. As is declared in another verse: **"He only has authority over those who take him as a friend and associate others with Allah"**. (Surat an-Nahl: 100)

In the Qur'an, the line to be taken by believers against Satan's unfounded allegations is thus prescribed:

If Satan tempts you, seek refuge in Allah. He is All-Hearing, All-Seeing. As for those who believe, when they are troubled by visitors from Satan, they have but to remember and they shall immediately see the light. (Surat al-A'raf: 200-201)

As long as they do not take refuge with Allah, those who listen to Satan's whispers will not be able to see the truth and will lead a life without reason. Allah has informed them that Satan will set up cunning traps but that these traps will be flimsy. And as we saw from the verses above, He has told people how to escape from these traps. A wise person immediately accepts the word of Allah and finds the right path. Those with frail understanding lead themselves to destruction by allowing themselves to be fooled by Satan's deceits. They disregard Allah's verses and, instead of Heaven, accept the life of Hell to which Satan drags them.

DISTRUSTING GOD

Another very important factor that clouds people's minds is their distrust of Allah, in other words not submitting to the fate Allah has decreed for them. One who doesn't trust Allah has forgotten that Allah has infinite wisdom and controls every situation and every creature in the universe. And because of this, as with all the other factors that veil the mind, he cannot analyse things clearly or fully see realities.

However, Allah watches over and protects all beings.

Whether they are aware of this or not, Allah creates events according to a decree and with these events He tests people. So, Allah creates every event a person faces throughout his life with a motive and for a good reason. This is how Allah warns people on this matter:

Allah alone has knowledge of what the heavens and the earth conceal; to Him all things shall be returned. So worship Him and put your trust in Him. Your Lord is not unaware of what you do. (Surah Hud: 123)

... It may be that you hate something when it is good for you and it may be that you love something when it is bad for you. Allah knows and you do not know. (Surat al-Baqara: 216)

One who believes these verses and comprehends that behind every incident there is a hidden motive and benefit for him, is one who has trust in Allah. Even if he faces a situation, which at first sight seems to his disadvantage, he knows that this will bring him good in this world and in the next and he acts on this knowledge. Because he evaluates incidents with full trust in Allah, his reasoning and judgement are in perfect shape, and as a result he can make sensible evaluations. On the other hand, one who has no faith in Allah forgets that Allah creates events in order to test him and so becomes totally distant from rationalism.

We can explain the great difference between these two people with an example. Let's say that a factory goes on fire and the owner of the factory forgets that this situation is controlled by Allah and doesn't think that there must be a benefit in this situation for him, so he begins to distrust Allah. And, one who doesn't trust Allah cannot think straight or take the necessary precautions or in any other way, act sensibly. For example, not being calm and composed can cause the otherwise extinguishable fire to grow. He loses time by being panic and grief-stricken and making a fuss instead of putting out the fire, saving his property, or calling the fire brigade. After the fire, instead of taking measures against future fires so that it won't ever happen again, he occupies himself with useless thoughts, such as "how and why did it happen, I wish it had not happened, or if I had done so-and-so it wouldn't have happened".

One, who trusts Allah, never becomes hopeless or sad, even if he loses everything he has. This person knows that Allah can take away a blessing He gave and that He does this to test people's trust in Him. With a clear consciousness, he tries to take care of the damage as soon as possible and takes the most swift and sensible precautions. He doesn't waste his time in panicking, worrying, or losing hope. Furthermore, without losing any time after such an event, he tries to make up for the damage by taking the most effective precautions possible so that it will not recur.

When it comes to the property he has lost, because he knows that the only owner of wealth is Allah, he is peaceful and at ease. He trusts Allah with all his heart and he prays for Him to give him more than what he has lost. And he is happy to know that he will be rewarded much more for his trust in Allah in the Hereafter.

Our Prophet (saas) explained this issue in the following example, *"If you put your whole trust in Allah, as you ought, He most certainly will satisfy your needs, as He satisfies those of the birds. They come out hungry in the morning, but return full to their nests."* (Tirmidhi)

SENTIMENTALITY AND ROMANTICISM

Romanticism is a way of life to which ignorant people see no objection; rather it is a way of life they like and encourage. They believe that, by looking at things romantically, life is enriched, as it is made much more colourful and interesting. For this reason, many movies, novels, and poems are given a romantic edge and romanticists try to make people believe that romanticism has a unique charm. However, the effect this has on people is to block their minds and prevent them from thinking logically and in a balanced way. This is because, romanticism totally disfavours reason. It is a way of life that leads people to ignore realities, live in a fantasy world, and think emotionally instead of reasonably.

One who submits himself to his emotions rather than his reason, who allows his emotions to guide him, can neither think realistically nor act logically. Let's consider the individual who has given himself up to jealousy—an attitude considered unacceptable by the teachings of the Quran. He will make aggressive outbursts as he can no longer analyse the situation he is in nor can he evaluate others rationally. In like manner, someone who lets his anger get the better of him cannot think clearly and may do something he will later regret.

Similarly, one who becomes depressed as a result of romanticism is totally distanced from rational thinking. As a result of the state he is in, he can see only the negative sides of things and becomes plunged in melancholy.

The foul behaviour that is evinced as a result of romanticism all have one point in common: they are the result of being far from Allah's religion and His book. This distance leads a person into absolute loss, because it is not possible for him to advance, achieve anything useful, or prevent something harmful where the ability to reason has been lost as a result of not obeying Allah's commands.

The destruction that lies behind the suicides, drug abuse, assault, or murders that occupy a large portion of the global news media is caused by romanticism and by being over-emotional. People become so apt to ignore the path of reason that they can easily destroy their own or others' lives or property. All the reasons they give to justify themselves have emotional factors at the root. For example, there are people who become upset at a harmless joke and kill as a result. Or, there are students who cannot get into a university, even though they have studied for months, and who try to commit suicide. Such people as cannot break away from their ambitions and who are so averse to reasonable conduct that they cannot even see other opportunities ahead of them, can make such irrational decisions under the influence of their emotions and then act upon these decisions.

Every step one takes under the influence of romanticism and with no reason being brought to bear will bring about an absolute loss. That is because romanticism is a belief of ignorant people that distances them from religion, and in turn from the real meaning of life. This way of life, which leads the individual into a life of hardship, is completely opposite to the way of thinking and morals laid down in the Qur'an by Allah.

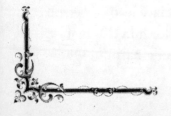

EXAMPLES OF THOUGHTLESSNESS IN EVERYDAY LIFE

As we saw in the earlier sections, one who cannot use his wisdom is at a great loss both in this world and the next. However, it would not be right to assess this loss only in terms of spirituality. A person also faces various hardships, discomfort, and losses caused by thoughtlessness in his daily life.

So, in this section we will explain the seriousness of this danger by providing examples of the kind of thoughtlessness that dogs the unintelligent person throughout his life.

IMPRUDENCE OF A THOUGHTLESS PERSON

In newspapers and television, we witness many occurrences that come about as a result of a lack of caution. And there is no end to these happenings. And many people make similar mistakes themselves, even though they read about them in the newspapers. We regularly come across a number of people who are go to sleep holding a cigarette and burn their homes down, whose children fall from balconies, whose fingers get caught in factory machinery, and so on and so forth. Without a doubt such examples of thoughtlessness are daily events experienced in societies that have strayed from religion. These people cannot make accurate predictions on how an event will develop after a few phases. Similarly, they cannot draw wise conclusions from their past experiences which they may be able to use in the future. Because they cannot appreciate the value of the means they have to hand, they cannot take sound precautions to prevent possible dangers.

Let us list some of the accidents and dangerous incidents that come about as a result of the imprudence of one who doesn't use his mind:

A thoughtless person tries to figure out how to use new equipment by experimenting with it, instead of using the manual or learning from someone who is acquainted with it. He doesn't see anything wrong in the rough handling of fragile parts or fiddling with buttons he doesn't know the use for on electronic items, such as a stereo set, or on a delicate device such as a computer. For this reason, he usually breaks brand new equipment without ever using it.

He doesn't see any harm in giving a child small pieces of plastic, which he can swallow, to play with. He begins to think of the inappropriateness of this behaviour when the child starts choking and needs to be taken to the hospital.

A thoughtless person tries to carry furniture made up of two or three pieces in one go and generally drops them all, half way. He cannot calculate that these need to be carried one by one.

A thoughtless person cannot imagine the damaging effect the sun will have on the human body. He harms his skin by staying out in the sun for longer than necessary, and sometimes even for hours on end. Because of the sun, his skin begins to swell up and deep wounds appear on his skin. He becomes nauseated and has a headache. Although he experiences these troubles every summer, he repeats the same mistake the next summer because he doesn't draw on his wisdom.

Moreover, he doesn't see any harm in playing with stray cats or dogs, which may be diseased for all he knows. In fact, most cases of diseases, such as rabies are the result of such imprudence.

Such a person is not sensitive to sudden smells or noises. He doesn't realize the significance of such things, even if he does realize it, he doesn't pay attention to them, either because of his unconcerned nature or because he cannot think of the dangers that may ensue. However, his house could burn down or he could be poisoned, because he cannot sense danger in the smell of gas or he may be faced with a fire because he doesn't respond to the smell of burning in time.

He injures himself by careless behaviour, such as plugging a wet plug into an outlet. He often suffers electric shocks because he changes the light bulb or does electronic repairs without shutting down the power.

He chops food very hastily with a very sharp knife. Because he doesn't calculate the possible injury, he cuts his finger.

Because he empties the dishwater with wet hands, the plates slip from his hand. And because he attempts to pick up the broken pieces with his hands he cuts himself.

He doesn't hesitate to open the door to a stranger and even invite him in. As a result, he is assaulted or his house is burgled.

By placing a hot pan on a glass table, he may cause it to crack. Or by placing a teapot on a wooden table he damages the surface.

When he is going on a road trip, he doesn't think to take preventative measures in case his car breaks down. Even if he does think of doing so, his arrangements are barely adequate. If he fills up the fuel tank, he forgets to take a spare tyre or check the water or the oil in the car.

He leaves everything to the last minute. For example, even when he has to catch his plane, he doesn't pack his luggage or run his errands till the last minute. Let's say his house is an hour away from the airport; he doesn't leave until there are only twenty minutes left. Even if he leaves on time, because he hasn't planned how to get there, he cannot find a cab or, even if he finds a cab, because he hasn't foreseen a traffic jam, he loses time and misses his flight. He experiences such mishaps all the time, but he still doesn't give up his indifference or think of wise precautions.

When he is carrying things, he doesn't think to remove anything that he could step on or bump into. He realizes his mistake only when he stumbles across obstacles or when he bumps into something while he is carrying something heavy.

He doesn't see the danger in placing an object on the edge of a coffee table, or other such piece of furniture from which it can fall and break with the slightest impact.

A THOUGHTLESS PERSON'S UNDERSTANDING OF ART AND AESTHETICS

Generally, people have a standard understanding of art and aesthetics. They apply the things they have learned from an early age throughout their lives. They apply whatever is thought to be fashionable at the time. But they don't apply their wisdom and try to produce something new. Their taste in art is completely based on imitation. Such people as are lacking in wisdom cannot come up with anything unique that they thought of themselves, even if they achieve a certain technical success with the things they imitate.

They especially use classical models in decorating their environment. We could make a list of the details of decorative styles people generally use.

As a thoughtless person doesn't use his time wisely, it takes him months to redecorate his house. Even the painting and cleaning of a small house goes on for months on end. He cannot evolve ways of doing tasks practically and efficiently.

One who doesn't apply his wisdom doesn't have any special interest in art or decoration; he can live without making any changes in his house for years. When he does eventually decide to make some changes, the first thing he thinks of is to change the fabric of the couches. He has no conception of moving the furniture around or in any other way making his surroundings more pleasant.

Even if he has a lot of opportunities, he cannot use them wisely. Even if he buys the most expensive, highest quality furniture, he cannot position it with any attempt at artistry.

Even if he succeeds in decorating his living space pleasantly, he fails to make it a relaxed, comfortable, and a healthy place to live in at the same time.

He cannot use his intelligence in the placing of his furniture. He places breakable, glass vases at points where people can easily bump into them. Similarly, he doesn't see any harm in using sharp and pointed objects as decorative pieces, and he places them where people can easily come into contact with them and hurt themselves.

He cannot get rid of anything, even though he has too many things. He tries to use old and new items at the same time. With every new item he purchases, he crowds his house and his house becomes even gloomier. He cannot realize the confusion that is created and is himself not disturbed by living in a gloomy place.

The things we listed thus far are only a few examples of how lack of wisdom reflects on daily life. But obviously, it is not possible to limit the hardship and damage thoughtlessness causes to people. One, who shuts his mind, will experience similar difficulties and hardship continuously till the end of his life. The only way to eliminate them, as has been explained from the beginning of the book, is to submit oneself to the clear mind with which religion rewards us. Thereby, wisdom, with the ease it brings, will rule a person's existence so that he may live a life of peace and beauty.

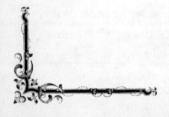

THE LOSSES THOUGHTLESSNESS BRINGS WITH IT

The biggest loss caused by thoughtlessness, without a doubt, is the distancing of people from Allah's religion. People who move further away from religion also move further from Heaven and drift into a life of infinite Hell. The thoughtlessness of these people show them the right things as wrong, the wrong things as right, for which reason they think that the real life is the life in this world and they see the real life of the Hereafter as very remote. As long as they are in this world they do not try to earn Allah's approval and His Heaven, and do not reckon that the torments of Hell will affect them. When they are faced with realities in the Hereafter, they voice their regret by saying: "We wish we had been wise" and they admit the huge loss thoughtlessness has caused them. This is how the Qur'an alludes to their regret:

And the Day Hell is brought near, that Day man will remember his deeds; but how will the remembrance help him? He will say, "Oh! If only I had been charitable in my lifetime!" (Surat al-Fajr: 23-24)

If only you could see them when they are standing before the Fire and saying, "Oh! If only we could be sent back again, we would not deny the Signs of our Lord and we would be true believers". (Surat al-An'am: 27)

They will say, "If only we had really listened and un-

derstood, we would not now have been the heirs of Hell." (Surat al-Mulk: 10)

The conclusion that should be reached from all of this is that thoughtlessness is a great misfortune that leads a person into Hell. And Hell is a place of torment where it is not even possible to die and so escape from it. This reality is definite enough and so much unbearable that no one may say, "Nothing will happen to me". The Qur'an mentions in detail the unbelievers in Hell in which there is heavy sighing, whose skin is renewed every time it is burned off, and who cannot find anything other than boiling water and scalding pus when they are thirsty.

Furthermore, one who doesn't use his mind should start thinking of the blessings of Heaven he will be deprived of, too. Before unreasoning people face Hell, they will be aware of the beauty of Heaven and see the joy believers experience as they are given the good news of Heaven. Knowing that believers are enjoying themselves on couches in mansions with rivers flowing under them will also leave a deep and painful mark of regret on the hearts of thoughtless people.

These are the losses thoughtlessness brings in the Hereafter. People distanced from religion because of their thoughtlessness try to enjoy worldly blessings by abandoning the Hereafter. But they cannot achieve what they want here either. They suffer material and spiritual losses throughout their lives. Firstly, they are untrusting of Allah, which is brought about by not submitting to Allah and His decree, and as a result of this they live in a state of unease. They lead lives of continual worry about the future, fear of losing what they have, anxiety about becoming destitute, grief at separation from loved ones, and becoming humiliated in others' eyes.

Because they don't live by the teachings of the Qur'an, they can never be close friends with anyone in the real sense; they cannot comprehend the beauty of real love, respect, loyalty, and many other moral virtues. As they don't live according to the Qur'an, they experience the difficulties of an ignorant system. Regret constantly rules their lives; they are always complaining about what they did the day before or even an hour before and keep voicing their regret.

Because they don't use their reason they cannot speak well or wisely. They talk for hours but still can't sort things out; they cannot take rapid precautions, and come up with rational solutions. Unable to see the beauty and refinement of others, they cannot express their appreciation of them. They can neither enjoy the subtleties of art and aesthetics nor can they develop practical innovations. They cannot give up their traditional way of living and their habits; they cannot renew themselves or evolve.

The state of thoughtless people is thus illustrated in the Qur'an:

> **Allah uses another metaphor: take a man who is deaf and dumb, unable to do anything, a burden on his master; no matter where he directs him he returns with empty hands. Is he as good as someone who commands justice and is on the right path? (Surat an-Nahl: 76)**

Without a doubt, this example expresses the state a thoughtless person is in. Since a thoughtless person, as declared in the verse, is someone who has no power over anything and, as well as not being of any benefit to himself, he is a burden to those around him. For this reason, the person in question has to live his life in a state of deprivation. Allah informs us of the state of thoughtless people in another verse:

None can believe except with Allah's permission. He places a blight on those who do not use their reason. (Surah Yunus: 100)

Moreover, thoughtless people form thoughtless communities. As a result of being far from religion, thoughtless communities are wracked with confusion, oppression, injustice, animosity, violence, and intolerance; theirs is basically an environment where every kind of negativity exists. As a result of their thoughtlessness, people cannot appreciate Allah's power and hence do not fear Him. And in a society where Allah is not feared, any kind of offence can be committed. People can easily kill others, abuse their rights, or turn to larceny and fraud. Because compassion and kindness are at a low, they indulge in any kind of wrongdoing.

So these are the summaries of some of the damage thoughtlessness causes in this world. For this reason, thoughtlessness is not a state that any individual should needlessly accept. Every human being should think of the obstacles blocking wisdom, should make every effort to try to rid himself of them, so that he may have the beautiful existence made possible by wisdom in this world and the next.

EXAMPLES OF THOUGHTLESSNESS IN THE QUR'AN

The Qur'an cites numerous examples of unreasoning human behaviour throughout history. Without a doubt learning about these examples will help one to comprehend the costs of thoughtlessness and to avoiding its consequences.

QARUN, THE OWNER OF TREASURES

Allah's giving Qarun, one of the people of Musa (as), great wealth is thus described in the Qur'an:

> Qarun was one of the people of Musa but he lorded it over them. We gave him such treasures, that their very keys would have weighed down a band of strong men. When his people said to him, "Do not gloat. Allah does not love people who gloat. Seek rather the abode of the Hereafter with what Allah has given you, without forgetting your share in this world. And do good as Allah has been good to you. And do not seek to cause corruption in the land. Allah does not love corrupters". (Surat al-Qasas: 76-77)

As is seen in the above verses, his people warn him not to forget that it is Allah Who has given him all this wealth, to thank Allah, and use his wealth in a way that would please Allah. But, Qarun grew arrogant and insisted that this wealth had been given to him because he possessed a certain knowledge.

He said, "I have only been given these riches because of the knowledge I have". Did he not know that before him Allah had destroyed generations with far greater strength than his and far more possessions? The evil-doers shall not be questioned about their sins. (Surat al-Qasas: 78)

Qarun's fascination with wealth and thinking he possessed it because of himself was thoughtless behaviour, since the only real owner of wealth is Allah: He can give wealth to whomever He wills, whenever He wants and take it away whenever He desires. After Allah makes His decision, neither a person's knowledge, wealth, nor possessions can change this decision.

Here is where Qarun's thoughtlessness was exposed. He acted with arrogance, thinking that his treasures would be able to save him in the face of Allah's warning and punishment. Instead of thanking Allah by using this wealth in order to please Him, he tried to gain the respect of others with his possessions.

Qarun's thoughtless behaviour exposed the other thoughtless people in his tribe, who looked at Qarun in the midst of his ostentatious wealth envied him and wanted to be in his place. People with wisdom, on the other hand, condemned their behaviours by reminding them that meriting Allah's approval was much better than all the magnificence and richness of the world:

He went out among his people in his finery. Those who desired the life of the world said, "Oh! If only we had the same as Qarun has been given! What immense good fortune he possesses". But those who had been given knowledge said, "Woe to you! Allah's reward is better for those who believe and act rightly. But only

the steadfast will obtain it". (Surat al-Qasas: 79-80)

Finally, because of his foolish arrogance, Allah obliterated both Qarun and his wealth. Neither his riches, nor the other things he claimed to possess could save him from this punishment. Those who had longed the day before, to be in Qarun's place as a result of being deluded by the adornment of the world, now realized how wrong they had been when they saw what happened to Qarun:

We caused the earth to swallow up both him and his house. There was no one to come to his aid, besides Allah, and he was unable to defend himself. Those who had longed to take his place the day before woke up saying, "Allah gives abundantly to any of His servants He wills and sparingly to whom He pleases. If Allah had not shown great kindness to us, we would have been swallowed up as well. Ah! Truly, the unbelievers shall never be successful". As for the abode of the Hereafter—We shall grant it to those who do not seek to exalt themselves in this world or to cause corruption in it. The successful outcome is for those who believe. (Surat al-Qasas: 81-83)

OWNERS OF THE GARDEN

People who are mentioned as owners of the garden in the Qur'an, fell into a similar error as that of Qarun, being guilty of thoughtless behaviour. They also failed to remember that the garden they owned was a blessing given to them by Allah. This is how their situation is mentioned in the Qur'an:

We have afflicted them as We afflicted the owners of the garden when they swore that they would pluck the

fruits the next morning, without saying the redeeming words, "If Allah wills". (Surat al-Qalam: 17-18)

This is the point where the owners of the garden were thoughtless, because no one can ever be definitely sure of what will happen in the future. Allah can put a person in an unexpected situation or a very different environment, whenever He wills. For this reason, the best and wisest thing to do in this situation is to be aware that one can only do something if Allah permits, and to ask Allah's permission. The Qur'an lays down how one should behave in such a situation:

Never say about anything, "I am doing that tomorrow", without adding "If Allah wills". Remember your Lord when you forget, and say, "Hopefully my Lord will guide me to something closer to the Truth". (Surat al-Kahf: 23-24)

The mistake made by the owners of the garden in this situation, was to forget that the owner and ruler of everything is Allah. When they went there early in the morning, they clearly saw that they had been greatly mistaken and now saw the seriousness of their thoughtlessness. To make them understand that the real possessor of power and wealth was Himself alone, Allah sent a plague upon their garden and dried the crops from their roots:

So a visitation from your Lord came upon it while they slept and in the morning it was like burnt land stripped bare. (Surat al-Qalam: 19-20)

The owners of the garden were talking among themselves, as they were about to go their garden in the morning, they voiced their greed in worldly goods as:

In the morning they called out to one another, "Leave

early for your garden if you want to pick the fruit". So
they set off, quietly saying to one another, "Do not let
any poor man into it today while you are there". They
left early, intent on carrying out their scheme. (Surat al-
Qalam: 21-25)

So, this was another mistake they made. When they voiced
their worldly greed, they forgot that Allah was a witness to it.
They thought that by going to their garden early, they could
avoid running into poor people. However, once Allah wills
something, they don't have the power to prevent it from happening, whatever they do. As they had been extremely greedy
about the crops they were going to harvest, when they saw what
had happened to their garden they were baffled and thought
they had come to the wrong place. But, later on they realized
that the reason for this was because they had not been suffi-
ciently grateful to Allah, and they began to condemn themselves:

But when they saw it, they said, "We must have lost our
way. No, the truth is we are destitute!" The best of them
said, "Did I not say to you, 'Why do you not glorify
Allah?'" They said, "Glory be to our Lord! Truly we
have been wrongdoers". They turned to face each other
in mutual accusation. They said, "Woe to us! We were
indeed transgressors. Maybe our Lord will give us
something better than this in exchange. We entreat our
Lord". (Surat al-Qalam: 26-32)

THE PROPHET NUH (AS)'S SON
Prophet Nuh (as) invited his people to believe in Allah, but
except for a small group of people, they didn't accept his pleas.

Then Allah informed Nuh (as) that He would send down a disaster to destroy them:

It was revealed to Nuh: "None of your people are going
to believe except for those who have already believed,
so do not be distressed at what they do. Build the Ark
under Our supervision and as We reveal, and do not
plead with Me concerning the wrongdoers. They shall
be drowned". (Surah Hud: 36-37)

The Prophet Nuh (as) built an ark as he was told by Allah in
the above verse. Then, he brought believers and his family on to
this ark at Allah's command.

When Our will was done, and water bubbled up from
the earth, We said to Nuh, "Load into the Ark a pair of
every species, and your family—except for those already doomed—and all who believe". But those who
believed with him were only a few. He said, "Embark
in it. In the name of Allah it shall set sail and cast an-
chor! Truly my Lord is Ever-Forgiving, and Most
Merciful". (Surah Hud: 40-41)

However, Nuh (as)'s son didn't board the ark and chose to
stay with the unbelievers. Nuh (as), who knew that Allah would
drown them, warned his son to board the ark and not to stay
with the unbelievers. However, his son insisted, saying that he
would take refuge on a mountain and that the mountain would
save him from this flood disaster:

It sailed with them through mountainous waves, and
Nuh called out to his son, who had kept himself apart,
"My son! Come on board with us. Do not stay with the
unbelievers!" He said, "I will take refuge on a mountain; It will protect me from the flood". He said, "There

is no protection from Allah's judgement today, except
for those He has mercy on". The waves surged in between them and he was among the drowned. It was
said, "Earth, swallow up your waters!" and, "Heaven,
hold back your rain!" The water subsided and His will
was done. The Ark came to land on al-Judi. And it was
said, "Away with the wrongdoers!" (Surah Hud: 42-44)

Without a doubt, it was not possible for Nuh's (as) son to escape from the great waves and the mountain could not save him.
The thoughtless error Nuh (as)'s son fell into at this point was
not comprehending that no one but Allah could save him from
this calamity that He had sent down. Because, as it was Allah
Who created the waves, He also created the mountains and it
was He Who subjected them to Him. After Allah wishes to destroy an individual or a community, there is no power or shelter
that can defy Him.

In fact, Nuh (as) reminded his son of the truth by saying,
**"There is no protection from Allah's judgement today except
for those He has mercy on"** but his son did not take this important advice into consideration. Even though he was warned, he
did not obey Allah's messenger and, as a result of his thoughtlessness, he received his punishment by drowning under the
waves.

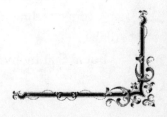

CONCLUSION

Those who are regretful in the Hereafter because they didn't use their reason as they were supposed to in this world are mentioned by the Quran as saying: **"If only we had really listened and understood, we would not now have been the heirs of Hell." (Surat al-Mulk: 10)**

Without a doubt, if a person thinks that such a consequence is also possible in his own case, it will enable him to be fearful and apprehend many things while there is still time. If a person in this situation ends up in Hell, he will most likely think with regret that even although his conscience had made him see things clearly in the world, possibly after numerous reminders, and despite there being no obstacles in his path, he still turned away from the way of intelligence.

However, by that time he is in Hellfire, where it is impossible for him to go back and compensate for his situation...

When he was in the world, he was reminded of Allah's punishment, but he didn't listen to these warnings because of his arrogance...

By saying "In any case there is a long life ahead of me, I can compensate for it in the future", he always delayed doing the right thing...

The wealth, beauty, or knowledge he possessed in the world gave him a feeling of greatness and prevented him from obeying Allah...

But at that moment there is nothing he can do to save himself from the fire and punishment; he is in a state of helplessness...

And whatever he does now, he can never get rid of the regret that he feels deep inside and he will constantly complain about his own thoughtlessness...

So, for a person to think, while he is still in this world, that he may face such a situation will result in his feeling deep regret there and then. In order not to say these words or words like these in Hellfire, he will decide to abide by his conscience from then on. When he consults his conscience, he will come across little and big things that everyone delays, or disregards, thinking them insignificant, or doesn't do, even if they know they are the right things to do. And it is possible for everyone to compensate for all these things right now.

If you ask anyone "Is it wiser to do this soul searching when full of regret in Hellfire, or now when there is still a chance to make up for it?" any sincere person would definitely say, "Of course now, in fact, right this second." Then he will turn his mind to trying to make up for all the unjust things he has done so far, without further delay.

In fact, this is the wisest action to take. Imagining oneself in the midst of Hellfire, even for a second, is enough for anyone to reach this sincere decision and act by his conscience. It is really easy for a person who trusts in and relies on Allah to make up for all his thoughtless and unjust behaviour till that moment. In the following verse, Allah informs people of the simplicity of this:

Say: "My servants, you who have transgressed against yourselves, do not despair of the mercy of Allah. Truly Allah forgives all wrong actions. He is the Ever-Forgiving, the Most Merciful". (Surat az-Zumar: 53)

However, a person should make haste in these matters and

not wait for hardship or death before he uses his reason. Allah reminds people in this verse that they need to act without wasting any time:

Turn to your Lord and submit to Him before punishment comes upon you, for then you cannot be helped. Follow the best that has been sent down to you from your Lord before the punishment comes upon you suddenly, when you are not expecting it. (Surat az-Zumar: 54-55)

It shouldn't be forgotten that one who sees the truth by consulting his conscience can make amends for the situation he is in. But, anyone who insists on not using his reason will definitely face the divine ire, having been led into regrettable acts that cannot be compensated for. In the following verse, the regret such people voice in the Hellfire is thus alluded to:

"... Alas: I have disobeyed Allah, and scoffed at His revelations!" (Surat az-Zumar: 56)

So this was what was intended in this book—to encourage people to do whatever they can right now in order not to face such a loss. With this purpose in mind, wisdom and thoughtlessness have been compared right from the beginning of the book and readers have been informed of the relative gains and losses. And at the end of the book it has been recalled once more, that thoughtlessness distances people from faith and, because of this, leads them into the torments of Hell. On the other hand, wisdom brings people to the blessings of Heaven. In order not to live with the guilt of thoughtlessness and a lack of conscience, everyone is invited once more to use his reason and find the right path.

THE DECEPTION OF EVOLUTION

Darwinism, in other words the theory of evolution, was put forward with the aim of denying the fact of creation, but is in truth nothing but failed, unscientific nonsense. This theory, which claims that life emerged by chance from inanimate matter, was invalidated by the scientific evidence of clear "design" in the universe and in living things. In this way, science confirmed the fact that Allah created the universe and the living things in it. The propaganda carried out today in order to keep the theory of evolution alive is based solely on the distortion of the scientific facts, biased interpretation, and lies and falsehoods disguised as science.

Yet this propaganda cannot conceal the truth. The fact that the theory of evolution is the greatest deception in the history of science has been expressed more and more in the scientific world over the last 20-30 years. Research carried out after the 1980s in particular has revealed that the claims of Darwinism are totally unfounded, something that has been stated by a large number of scientists. In the United States in particular, many scientists from such different fields as biology, biochemistry and paleontology recognize the invalidity of Darwinism and employ the concept of intelligent design to account for the origin of life. This "intelligent design" is a scientific expression of the fact that Allah created all living things.

We have examined the collapse of the theory of evolution and the proofs of creation in great scientific detail in many of our works, and are still continuing to do so. Given the enormous importance of this subject, it will be of great benefit to summarize it here.

The Scientific Collapse of Darwinism

Although this doctrine goes back as far as ancient Greece, the theory of evolution was advanced extensively in the nineteenth century. The most important development that made it the top topic of the world of science was Charles Darwin's *The Origin of Species*, published in 1859. In this book, he denied that Allah created different living species on Earth separately, for he claimed that all living beings had a common ancestor and had diversified over time through small changes. Darwin's theory was not based on any concrete scientific finding; as he also accepted, it was just an "assumption". Moreover, as Darwin confessed in the long chapter of his book titled "Difficulties of the Theory", the theory failed in the face of many critical questions.

Darwin invested all of his hopes in new scientific discoveries, which he expected to solve these difficulties. However, contrary to his expectations, scientific findings expanded the dimensions of these difficulties. The defeat of Darwinism in the face of science can be reviewed under three basic topics:

1) The theory cannot explain how life originated on Earth.

2) No scientific finding shows that the "evolutionary mechanisms" proposed by the theory have any evolutionary power at all.

3) The fossil record proves the exact opposite of what the theory suggests.

In this section, we will examine these three basic points in general outlines:

The First Insurmountable Step: The Origin of Life

The theory of evolution posits that all living species evolved from a single living cell that emerged on the primitive Earth 3.8 billion years ago. How a single cell could generate millions of complex living species and, if such an evolution really occurred, why traces of it cannot be observed in the fossil record are some of the questions that the theory cannot answer. However, first and foremost, we need to ask: How did this "first cell" originate?

Since the theory of evolution denies creation and any kind of supernatural intervention, it maintains that the "first cell" originated coincidentally within the laws of nature, without any design, plan or arrangement. According to the theory, inanimate matter must have produced a living cell as a result of coincidences. Such a claim, however, is inconsistent with the most unassailable rules of biology.

"Life Comes from Life"

In his book, Darwin never referred to the origin of life. The primitive understanding of science in his time rested on the assumption that living beings had a very simple structure. Since medieval times, spontaneous generation, which asserts that non-living materials came together to form living organisms, had been widely accepted. It was commonly believed that insects came into being from food leftovers, and mice from wheat. Interesting experiments were conducted to prove this theory. Some wheat was placed on a dirty piece of cloth, and it was believed that mice would originate from it after a while.

Similarly, maggots developing in rotting meat was assumed to be evidence of spontaneous generation. However, it was later understood that worms did not appear on meat spontaneously, but were carried there by flies in the form of larvae, invisible to the naked eye.

Even when Darwin wrote *The Origin of Species*, the belief that bacteria could come into existence from non-living matter was widely accepted in the world of science.

However, five years after the publication of Darwin's book, Louis Pasteur announced his results after long studies and experiments, that disproved spontaneous generation, a cornerstone of Darwin's theory. In his triumphal lecture at the Sorbonne in 1864, Pasteur said: "Never will the doctrine of spontaneous generation recover from the mortal blow struck by this simple experiment."[1]

For a long time, advocates of the theory of evolution resisted these findings. However, as the development of science unraveled the complex structure of the cell of a living being, the idea that life could come into being coincidentally faced an even greater impasse.

Inconclusive Efforts in the Twentieth Century

The first evolutionist who took up the subject of the origin of life in the twentieth century was the renowned Russian biologist Alexander Oparin. With various theses he advanced in the 1930s, he tried to prove that a living cell could originate by coincidence. These studies, however, were doomed to failure, and Oparin had to make the following confession:

Unfortunately, however, the problem of the origin of the cell is perhaps the most obscure point in the whole study of the evolution of organisms.[2]

Evolutionist followers of Oparin tried to carry out experiments to solve this problem. The best known experiment was carried out by the American chemist Stanley Miller in 1953. Combining the gases he alleged to have existed in the primordial Earth's atmosphere in an experiment set-up, and adding energy to the mixture, Miller synthesized several organic molecules (amino acids) present in the structure of proteins.

Barely a few years had passed before it was revealed that this experiment, which was then presented as an important step in the name of evolution, was invalid, for the atmosphere used in the experiment was very different from the real Earth conditions.[3]

After a long silence, Miller confessed that the atmosphere medium he used was unrealistic.[4]

All the evolutionists' efforts throughout the twentieth century to explain the origin of life ended in failure. The geochemist Jeffrey Bada, from the San Diego Scripps Institute accepts this fact in an article published in *Earth* magazine in 1998:

> Today as we leave the twentieth century, we still face the biggest unsolved problem that we had when we entered the twentieth century: How did life originate on Earth?[5]

The Complex Structure of Life

The primary reason why the theory of evolution ended up in such a great impasse regarding the origin of life is that even those living organisms deemed to be the simplest have incredibly complex structures. The cell of a living thing is more complex than all of our man-made technological products. Today, even in the most developed laboratories of the world, a living cell cannot be produced by bringing organic chemicals together.

The conditions required for the formation of a cell are too great in quantity to be explained away by coincidences. The probability of proteins, the building blocks of a cell, being synthesized coincidentally, is 1 in 10^{950} for an average protein made up of 500 amino acids. In mathematics, a probability smaller than 1 over 10^{50} is considered to be impossible in practical terms.

The DNA molecule, which is located in the nucleus of a cell and which stores genetic information, is an incredible databank. If the information coded in DNA were written down, it would make a giant library consisting of an estimated 900 volumes of encyclopedias consisting of 500 pages each.

A very interesting dilemma emerges at this point: DNA can replicate itself only with the help of some specialized proteins (enzymes). However, the synthesis of these enzymes can be realized only by the information coded in DNA. As they both depend on each other, they have to exist at the same time for replication. This brings the scenario that life originated by itself to a deadlock. Prof. Leslie Orgel, an evolutionist of repute from the University of San Diego, California, confesses this fact in the September 1994 issue of the *Scientific American* magazine:

> It is extremely improbable that proteins and nucleic acids, both of which are structurally complex, arose spontaneously in the same place at the same time. Yet it also seems impossible to have one without the other. And so, at first glance, one might have to conclude that life could never, in fact, have originated

by chemical means.[6]

No doubt, if it is impossible for life to have originated from natural causes, then it has to be accepted that life was "created" in a supernatural way. This fact explicitly invalidates the theory of evolution, whose main purpose is to deny creation.

Imaginary Mechanisms of Evolution

The second important point that negates Darwin's theory is that both concepts put forward by the theory as "evolutionary mechanisms" were understood to have, in reality, no evolutionary power.

Darwin based his evolution allegation entirely on the mechanism of "natural selection". The importance he placed on this mechanism was evident in the name of his book: *The Origin of Species, By Means of Natural Selection...*

Natural selection holds that those living things that are stronger and more suited to the natural conditions of their habitats will survive in the struggle for life. For example, in a deer herd under the threat of attack by wild animals, those that can run faster will survive. Therefore, the deer herd will be comprised of faster and stronger individuals. However, unquestionably, this mechanism will not cause deer to evolve and transform themselves into another living species, for instance, horses.

Therefore, the mechanism of natural selection has no evolutionary power. Darwin was also aware of this fact and had to state this in his book *The Origin of Species*:

Natural selection can do nothing until favourable individual differences or variations occur.[7]

Lamarck's Impact

So, how could these "favourable variations" occur? Darwin tried to answer this question from the standpoint of the primitive understanding of science at that time. According to the French biologist Chevalier de Lamarck (1744-1829), who lived before Darwin, living creatures passed on the traits they acquired during their lifetime to the next generation. He asserted that these traits, which accumulated from one generation to another, caused new species to be formed. For instance, he claimed that giraffes evolved from antelopes; as they struggled to eat the leaves of high trees, their necks were extended from generation to generation.

Darwin also gave similar examples. In his book *The Origin of Species*, for instance, he said that some bears going into water to find food transformed themselves into whales over time.[8]

However, the laws of inheritance discovered by Gregor Mendel (1822-84) and verified by the science of genetics, which flourished in the twentieth century, utterly demolished the legend that acquired traits were passed on to subsequent generations. Thus, natural selection fell out of favour as an evolutionary mechanism.

Neo-Darwinism and Mutations

In order to find a solution, Darwinists advanced the "Modern Synthetic Theory", or as it is more commonly known, Neo-Darwinism, at the end of the 1930's. Neo-Darwinism added mutations, which are distortions formed in the genes of living beings due to such external factors as radiation or replication errors, as the "cause of favourable variations" in addition to natural mutation.

Today, the model that stands for evolution in the world is Neo-Darwinism. The theory maintains that millions of living beings formed as a result of a process whereby numerous complex organs of these organisms (e.g., ears, eyes, lungs, and wings) underwent "mutations", that is, genetic disorders. Yet, there is an outright scientific fact that totally undermines this theory: Mutations do not cause living beings to develop; on the contrary, they are always harmful.

The reason for this is very simple: DNA has a very complex structure, and random effects can only harm it. The American geneticist B.G. Ranganathan explains this as follows:

> First, genuine mutations are very rare in nature. Secondly, most mutations are harmful since they are random, rather than orderly changes in the structure of genes; any random change in a highly ordered system will be for the worse, not for the better. For example, if an earthquake were to shake a highly ordered structure such as a building, there would be a random change in the framework of the building which, in all probability, would not be an improvement.[9]

Not surprisingly, no mutation example, which is useful, that is, which is observed to develop the genetic code, has been observed so far. All mutations have proved to be harmful. It was understood that mutation, which is presented as an "evolutionary mechanism", is actually a genetic occurrence that harms living things, and leaves them disabled. (The most common effect of mutation on human beings is cancer.) Of course, a destructive mechanism cannot be an "evolutionary mechanism". Natural selection, on the other hand, "can do nothing by itself", as Darwin also accepted. This fact shows us that there is no "evolutionary mechanism" in nature. Since no evolutionary mechanism exists, no such any imaginary process called "evolution" could have taken place.

The Fossil Record: No Sign of Intermediate Forms

The clearest evidence that the scenario suggested by the theory of evolution did not take place is the fossil record.

According to this theory, every living species has sprung from a predecessor. A previously existing species turned into something else over time and all species have come into being in this way. In other words, this transformation proceeds gradually over millions of years.

Had this been the case, numerous intermediary species should have existed and lived within this long transformation period.

For instance, some half-fish/half-reptiles should have lived in the past which had acquired some reptilian traits in addition to the fish traits they already had. Or there should have existed some reptile-birds, which acquired some bird traits in addition to the reptilian traits they already had. Since these would be in a transitional phase, they should be disabled, defective, crippled living beings. Evolutionists refer to these imaginary creatures, which they believe to have lived in the past, as "transitional forms".

If such animals ever really existed, there should be millions and even billions of them in number and variety. More importantly, the remains of these strange creatures should be present in the fossil record. In *The Origin of Species,* Darwin explained:

> If my theory be true, numberless intermediate varieties, linking most closely all of the species of the same group together must assuredly have existed... Consequently, evidence of their former existence could be found only amongst fossil remains.[10]

Darwin's Hopes Shattered

However, although evolutionists have been making strenuous efforts to find fossils since the middle of the nineteenth century all over the world, no transitional forms have yet been uncovered. All of the fossils, contrary to the evolutionists' expectations, show that life appeared on Earth all of a sudden and fully-formed.

One famous British paleontologist, Derek V. Ager, admits this fact, even though he is an evolutionist:

> The point emerges that if we examine the fossil record in detail, whether at the level of orders or of species, we find—over and over again—not gradual evolution, but the sudden explosion of one group at the expense of another.[11]

This means that in the fossil record, all living species suddenly emerge as fully formed, without any intermediate forms in between. This is just the opposite of Darwin's assumptions. Also, this is very strong evidence that all living things are created. The only explanation of a living species emerging suddenly and complete in every detail without any evolutionary ancestor is that it was created. This fact is admitted also by the widely known evolutionist biologist Douglas Futuyma:

Creation and evolution, between them, exhaust the possible explanations for the origin of living things. Organisms either appeared on the earth fully developed or they did not. If they did not, they must have developed from pre-existing species by some process of modification. If they did appear in a fully developed state, they must indeed have been created by some omnipotent intelligence.[12]

Fossils show that living beings emerged fully developed and in a perfect state on the Earth. That means that "the origin of species", contrary to Darwin's supposition, is not evolution, but creation.

The Tale of Human Evolution

The subject most often brought up by advocates of the theory of evolution is the subject of the origin of man. The Darwinist claim holds that modern man evolved from ape-like creatures. During this alleged evolutionary process, which is supposed to have started 4-5 million years ago, some "transitional forms" between modern man and his ancestors are supposed to have existed. According to this completely imaginary scenario, four basic "categories" are listed:

1. *Australopithecus*
2. *Homo habilis*
3. *Homo erectus*
4. *Homo sapiens*

Evolutionists call man's so-called first ape-like ancestors *Australopithecus*, which means "South African ape". These living beings are actually nothing but an old ape species that has become extinct. Extensive research done on various *Australopithecus* specimens by two world famous anatomists from England and the USA, namely, Lord Solly Zuckerman and Prof. Charles Oxnard, shows that these apes belonged to an ordinary ape species that became extinct and bore no resemblance to humans.[13]

Evolutionists classify the next stage of human evolution as "*homo*", that is "man". According to their claim, the living beings in the *Homo* series are more developed than *Australopithecus*. Evolutionists devise a fanciful evolution scheme by arranging different fossils of these creatures in a particular order. This scheme is imaginary because it has never been proved that there is an evolutionary relation between these different classes. Ernst Mayr, one of the twentieth century's most important evolutionists, contends in his book *One Long Argument* that "particularly historical [puzzles] such as the origin of life or of *Homo sapiens*, are extremely difficult and may even resist a final, satisfying explanation."[14]

By outlining the link chain as *Australopithecus* > *Homo habilis* > *Homo erectus* > *Homo sapiens*, evolutionists imply that each of these species is one another's ancestor. However, recent findings of paleoanthropologists have revealed that *Australopithecus*, *Homo habilis*, and *Homo erectus* lived at different parts of the world at the same time.[15]

Moreover, a certain segment of humans classified as *Homo erectus* have lived up until very modern times. *Homo sapiens neandarthalensis* and *Homo sapiens sapiens* (modern man) co-existed in the same region.[16]

This situation apparently indicates the invalidity of the claim that they are ancestors of one another. A paleontologist from Harvard University, Stephen Jay Gould, explains this deadlock of the theory of evolution, although he is an evolution-ist himself:

> What has become of our ladder if there are three coexisting lineages of hominids (A. africanus, the robust australopithe-cines, and H. habilis), none clearly derived from another? Moreover, none of the three display any evolutionary trends during their tenure on earth.[17]

Put briefly, the scenario of human evolution, which is "up-held" with the help of various drawings of some "half ape, half human" creatures appearing in the media and course books, that is, frankly, by means of propaganda, is nothing but a tale with no scientific foundation.

Lord Solly Zuckerman, one of the most famous and respected scientists in the U.K., who carried out research on this subject for years and studied *Australopithecus* fossils for 15 years, finally concluded, despite being an evolutionist himself, that there is, in fact, no such family tree branching out from ape-like creatures to man.

Zuckerman also made an interesting "spectrum of science" ranging from those he considered scientific to those he considered unscientific. According to Zuckerman's spectrum, the most "sci-entific"-that is, depending on concrete data-fields of science are chemistry and physics. After them come the biological sciences and then the social sciences. At the far end of the spectrum, which is the part considered to be most "unscientific", are "extra-sensory perception"—concepts such as telepathy and sixth sense-and finally "human evolution". Zuckerman explains his reasoning:

> We then move right off the register of objective truth into those fields of presumed biological science, like extrasenso-

ry perception or the interpretation of man's fossil history, where to the faithful [evolutionist] anything is possible—and where the ardent believer [in evolution] is sometimes able to believe several contradictory things at the same time.[18]

The tale of human evolution boils down to nothing but the prejudiced interpretations of some fossils unearthed by certain people, who blindly adhere to their theory.

Darwinian Formula!

Besides all the technical evidence we have dealt with so far, let us now for once, examine what kind of a superstition the evolutionists have with an example so simple as to be understood even by children:

The theory of evolution asserts that life is formed by chance. According to this claim, lifeless and unconscious atoms came together to form the cell and then they somehow formed other living things, including man. Let us think about that. When we bring together the elements that are the building-blocks of life such as carbon, phosphorus, nitrogen and potassium, only a heap is formed. No matter what treatments it undergoes, this atomic heap cannot form even a single living being. If you like, let us formulate an "experiment" on this subject and let us examine on the behalf of evolutionists what they really claim without pronouncing loudly under the name "Darwinian formula":

Let evolutionists put plenty of materials present in the composition of living things such as phosphorus, nitrogen, carbon, oxygen, iron, and magnesium into big barrels. Moreover, let them add in these barrels any material that does not exist under normal conditions, but they think as necessary. Let them add in this mixture as many amino acids—which have no possibility of forming under natural conditions—and as many proteins—a single one of which has a formation probability of 10^{950}—as they like. Let them expose these mixtures to as much heat and moisture as they like. Let them stir these with whatever techno-logically developed device they like. Let them put the foremost scientists beside these barrels. Let these experts wait in turn be-side these barrels for billions, and even trillions of years. Let them be free to use all kinds of conditions they believe to be nec-essary for a human's formation. No matter what they do, they cannot produce from these barrels a human, say a professor that examines his cell structure under the electron microscope. They cannot produce giraffes, lions, bees, canaries, horses, dolphins, roses, orchids, lilies, carnations, bananas, oranges, apples, dates, tomatoes, melons, watermelons, figs, olives, grapes, peaches, peafowls, pheasants, multicoloured butterflies, or millions of other living beings such as these. Indeed, they could not obtain even a single cell of any one of them.

Briefly, unconscious atoms cannot form the cell by coming together. They cannot take a new decision and divide this cell into two, then take other decisions and create the professors who first invent the electron microscope and then examine their own cell structure under that microscope. Matter is an uncon-scious, lifeless heap, and it comes to life with Allah's superior creation.

The theory of evolution, which claims the opposite, is a total fallacy completely contrary to reason. Thinking even a lit-tle bit on the claims of tevolutionists discloses this reality, just as in the above example.

Technology in the Eye and the Ear

Another subject that remains unanswered by evolutionary theory is the excellent quality of perception in the eye and the ear.

Before passing on to the subject of the eye, let us briefly answer the question of how we see. Light rays coming from an object fall oppositely on the eye's retina. Here, these light rays are transmitted into electric signals by cells and reach a tiny spot at the back of the brain, the "center of vision". These electric signals are perceived in this center as an image after a series of processes. With this technical background, let us do some thinking.

The brain is insulated from light. That means that its inside is completely dark, and that no light reaches the place where it is located. Thus, the "center of vision" is never touched by light and may even be the darkest place you have ever known. However, you observe a luminous, bright world in this pitch darkness.

The image formed in the eye is so sharp and distinct that even the technology of the twentieth century has not been able to attain it. For instance, look at the book you are reading, your hands with which you are holding it, and then lift your head and look around you. Have you ever seen such a sharp and distinct image as this one at any other place? Even the most developed television screen produced by the greatest television producer in the world cannot provide such a sharp image for you. This is a three-dimensional, colored, and extremely sharp image. For more than 100 years, thousands of engineers have been trying to achieve this sharpness. Factories, huge premises were established, much research has been done, plans and designs have been made for this purpose. Again, look at a TV screen and the book you hold in your hands. You will see that there is a big difference in sharpness and distinction. Moreover, the TV screen shows you a two-dimensional image, whereas with your eyes, you watch a three-dimensional perspective with depth.

For many years, tens of thousands of engineers have tried to make a three-dimensional TV and achieve the vision quality of the eye. Yes, they have made a three-dimensional television system, but it is not possible to watch it without putting on special 3-D glasses; moreover, it is only an artificial three-dimension. The background is more blurred, the foreground appears like a paper setting. Never has it been possible to produce a sharp and distinct vision like that of the eye. In both the camera and the television, there is a loss of image quality.

Evolutionists claim that the mechanism producing this sharp and distinct image has been formed by chance. Now, if somebody told you that the television in your room was formed as a result of chance, that all of its atoms just happened to come together and make up this device that produces an image, what would you think? How can atoms do what thousands of people cannot?

If a device producing a more primitive image than the eye could not have been formed by chance, then it is very evident that the eye and the image seen by the eye could not have been formed by chance. The same situation applies to the ear. The outer ear picks up the available sounds by the auricle and directs them to the middle ear, the middle ear transmits the sound vibrations by intensifying them, and the inner ear sends these vibrations to the brain by translating them into electric signals. Just as with the eye, the act of hearing finalizes in the center of hearing in the brain.

The situation in the eye is also true for the ear. That is, the brain is insulated from sound just as it is from light. It does not let any sound in. Therefore, no matter how noisy is the outside, the inside of the brain is completely silent. Nevertheless, the sharpest sounds are perceived in the brain. In your completely silent brain, you listen to symphonies, and hear all of the noises in a crowded place. However, were the sound level in your brain was measured by a precise device at that moment, complete silence would be found to be prevailing there.

As is the case with imagery, decades of effort have been spent in trying to generate and reproduce sound that is faithful to the original. The results of these efforts are sound recorders, high-fidelity systems, and systems for sensing sound. Despite all of this technology and the thousands of engineers and experts who have been working on this endeavor, no sound has yet been obtained that has the same sharpness and clarity as the sound perceived by the ear. Think of the highest-quality hi-fi systems produced by the largest company in the music industry. Even in these devices, when sound is recorded some of it is lost; or when you turn on a hi-fi you always hear a hissing sound before the music starts. However, the sounds that are the products of the human body's technology are extremely sharp and clear. A human ear never perceives a sound accompanied by a hissing sound or with atmospherics as does a hi-fi; rather, it perceives sound exactly as it is, sharp and clear. This is the way it has been since the creation of man.

So far, no man-made visual or recording apparatus has been as sensitive and successful in perceiving sensory data as are the eye and the ear. However, as far as seeing and hearing are concerned, a far greater truth lies beyond all this.

To Whom Does the Consciousness That Sees and Hears Within the Brain Belong?

Who watches an alluring world in the brain, listens to symphonies and the twittering of birds, and smells the rose?

The stimulations coming from a person's eyes, ears, and nose travel to the brain as electro-chemical nerve impulses. In biology, physiology, and biochemistry books, you can find many details about how this image forms in the brain. However, you will never come across the most important fact: Who perceives these electro-chemical nerve impulses as images, sounds, odors, and sensory events in the brain? There is a consciousness in the brain that perceives all this without feeling any need for an eye, an ear, and a nose. To whom does this consciousness belong? Of course it does not belong to the nerves, the fat layer, and neurons comprising the brain. This is why Darwinist-materialists, who believe that everything is comprised of matter, cannot answer these questions.

For this consciousness is the spirit created by Allah, which needs neither the eye to watch the images nor the ear to hear the sounds. Furthermore, it does not need the brain to think.

Everyone who reads this explicit and scientific fact should ponder on Almighty Allah, and fear and seek refuge in Him, for He squeezes the entire universe in a pitch-dark place of a few cubic centimeters in a three-dimensional, colored, shadowy, and luminous form.

A Materialist Faith

The information we have presented so far shows us that the

theory of evolution is a incompatible with scientific findings. The theory's claim regarding the origin of life is inconsistent with science, the evolutionary mechanisms it proposes have no evolutionary power, and fossils demonstrate that the required intermediate forms have never existed. So, it certainly follows that the theory of evolution should be pushed aside as an unscientific idea. This is how many ideas, such as the Earth-centered universe model, have been taken out of the agenda of science throughout history.

However, the theory of evolution is kept on the agenda of science. Some people even try to represent criticisms directed against it as an "attack on science". Why?

The reason is that this theory is an indispensable dogmatic belief for some circles. These circles are blindly devoted to materialist philosophy and adopt Darwinism because it is the only materialist explanation that can be put forward to explain the workings of nature.

Interestingly enough, they also confess this fact from time to time. A well-known geneticist and an outspoken evolutionist, Richard C. Lewontin from Harvard University, confesses that he is "first and foremost a materialist and then a scientist":

> It is not that the methods and institutions of science somehow compel us accept a material explanation of the phenomenal world, but, on the contrary, that we are forced by our a priori adherence to material causes to create an apparatus of investigation and a set of concepts that produce material explanations, no matter how counter-intuitive, no matter how mystifying to the uninitiated. Moreover, that materialism is absolute, so we cannot allow a Divine Foot in the door.[19]

These are explicit statements that Darwinism is a dogma kept alive just for the sake of adherence to materialism. This dogma maintains that there is no being save matter. Therefore, it argues that inanimate, unconscious matter created life. It insists that millions of different living species (e.g., birds, fish, giraffes, tigers, insects, trees, flowers, whales, and human beings) originated as a result of the interactions between matter such as pouring rain, lightning flashes, and so on, out of inanimate matter. This is a precept contrary both to reason and science. Yet Darwinists continue to defend it just so as "not to allow a Divine Foot in the door".

Anyone who does not look at the origin of living beings with a materialist prejudice will see this evident truth: All living beings are works of a Creator, Who is All-Powerful, All-Wise, and All-Knowing. This Creator is Allah, Who created the whole universe from non-existence, designed it in the most perfect form, and fashioned all living beings.

The Theory of Evolution is the Most Potent Spell in the World

Anyone free of prejudice and the influence of any particular ideology, who uses only his or her reason and logic, will clearly understand that belief in the theory of evolution, which brings to mind the superstitions of societies with no knowledge of science or civilization, is quite impossible.

As explained above, those who believe in the theory of evolution think that a few atoms and molecules thrown into a huge vat could produce thinking, reasoning professors and university students; such scientists as Einstein and Galileo; such artists as Humphrey Bogart, Frank Sinatra and Luciano Pavarotti; as well as antelopes, lemon trees, and carnations. Moreover, as the scientists and professors who believe in this nonsense are educated people, it is quite justifiable to speak of this theory as "the most potent spell in history". Never before has any other belief or idea so taken away peoples' powers of reason, refused to allow them to think intelligently and logically and hidden the truth from them as if they had been blindfolded. This is an even worse and unbelievable blindness than the Egyptians worshipping the Sun God Ra, totem worship in some parts of Africa, the people of Saba worshipping the Sun, the tribe of Prophet Ibrahim (as) worshipping idols they had made with their own hands, or the people of the Prophet Musa (as) worshipping the Golden Calf.

In fact, Allah has pointed to this lack of reason in the Qur'an. In many verse, He reveals in many verses that some peoples' minds will be closed and that they will be powerless to see the truth. Some of these verses are as follows:

As for those who do not believe, it makes no difference to them whether you warn them or do not warn them, they will not believe. Allah has sealed up their hearts and hearing and over their eyes is a blindfold. They will have a terrible punishment. (Surat al-Baqara: 6-7)

... They have hearts with which they do not understand. They have eyes with which they do not see. They have ears with which they do not hear. Such people are like cattle. No, they are even further astray! They are the unaware. (Surat al-A`raf: 179)

Even if We opened up to them a door into heaven, and they spent the day ascending through it, they would only say: "Our eyesight is befuddled! Or rather we have been put under a spell!" (Surat al-Hijr: 14-15)

Words cannot express just how astonishing it is that this spell should hold such a wide community in thrall, keep people from the truth, and not be broken for 150 years. It is understandable that one or a few people might believe in impossible scenarios and claims full of stupidity and illogicality. However, "magic" is the only possible explanation for people from all over the world believing that unconscious and lifeless atoms suddenly decided to come together and form a universe that functions with a flawless system of organization, discipline, reason, and consciousness; a planet named Earth with all of its features so perfectly suited to life; and living things full of countless complex systems.

In fact, the Qur'an relates the incident of Prophet Musa and Pharaoh to show that some people who support atheistic philosophies actually influence others by magic. When Pharaoh was told about the true religion, he told Musa (as) to meet with his own magicians. When Musa (as) did so, he told them to demonstrate their abilities first. The verses continue:

He said: "You throw." And when they threw, they cast a spell on the people's eyes and caused them to feel great fear of them. They produced an extremely powerful magic. (Surat al-A`raf: 116)

As we have seen, Pharaoh's magicians were able to deceive everyone, apart from Musa (as) and those who believed in him. However, his evidence broke the spell, or "swallowed up what they had forged", as the verse puts it.

We revealed to Musa, "Throw down your staff." And it immediately swallowed up what they had forged. So the Truth took place and what they did was shown to be false. (Surat al-A`raf: 117-119)

As we can see, when people realized that a spell had been cast upon them and that what they saw was just an illusion, Pharaoh's magicians lost all credibility. In the present day too, unless those who, under the influence of a similar spell, believe in these ridiculous claims under their scientific disguise and spend their lives defending them, abandon their superstitious beliefs, they also will be humiliated when the full truth emerges and the spell is broken. In fact, Malcolm Muggeridge, an atheist philosopher and supporter of evolution, admitted he was worried by just that prospect:

> I myself am convinced that the theory of evolution, especially the extent to which it's been applied, will be one of the great jokes in the history books in the future. Posterity will marvel that so very flimsy and dubious an hypothesis could be accepted with the incredible credulity that it has.[20]

That future is not far off: On the contrary, people will soon see that "chance" is not a deity, and will look back on the theory of evolution as the worst deceit and the most terrible spell in the world. That spell is already rapidly beginning to be lifted from the shoulders of people all over the world. Many people who see its true face are wondering with amazement how they could ever have been taken in by it.

They said, "Glory be to You! We have no knowledge except what You have taught us.
You are the All-Knowing, the All-Wise."
(Surat al-Baqara: 32)

NOTES

1 Sidney Fox, Klaus Dose, *Molecular Evolution and The Origin of Life*, W.H. Freeman and Company, San Francisco, 1972, p. 4.

2 Alexander I. Oparin, *Origin of Life*, Dover Publications, NewYork, 1936, 1953 (reprint), p. 196.

3 "New Evidence on Evolution of Early Atmosphere and Life", *Bulletin of the American Meteorological Society*, vol 63, November 1982, p. 1328-1330.

4 Stanley Miller, *Molecular Evolution of Life: Current Status of the Prebiotic Synthesis of Small Molecules*, 1986, p. 7.

5 Jeffrey Bada, *Earth*, February 1998, p. 40.

6 Leslie E. Orgel, "The Origin of Life on Earth", *Scientific American*, vol. 271, October 1994, p. 78.

7 Charles Darwin, *The Origin of Species by Means of Natural Selection*, *The Modern Library*, New York, p. 127.

8 Charles Darwin, *The Origin of Species: A Facsimile of the First Edition*, Harvard University Press, 1964, p. 184.

9 B. G. Ranganathan, *Origins?*, Pennsylvania: The Banner Of Truth Trust, 1988, p. 7.

10 Charles Darwin, *The Origin of Species: A Facsimile of the First Edition*, Harvard University Press, 1964, p. 179.

11 Derek A. Ager, "The Nature of the Fossil Record", *Proceedings of the British Geological Association*, vol 87, 1976, p. 133.

12 Douglas J. Futuyma, *Science on Trial*, Pantheon Books, New York, 1983. p. 197.

13 Solly Zuckerman, *Beyond The Ivory Tower*, Toplinger Publications, New York, 1970, pp. 75-14; Charles E. Oxnard, "The Place of Australopithecines in Human Evolution: Grounds for Doubt", Nature, vol 258, p. 389.

14 "Could science be brought to an end by scientists' belief

that they have final answers or by society's reluctance to pay the bills?" *Scientific American*, December 1992, p. 20.

15 Alan Walker, *Science*, vol. 207, 7 March 1980, p. 1103; A. J. Kelso, Physical Antropology, 1st ed., J. B. Lipincott Co., New York, 1970, p. 221; M. D. Leakey, Olduvai Gorge, vol. 3, Cambridge University Press, Cambridge, 1971, p. 272.

16 Jeffrey Kluger, "Not So Extinct After All: The Primitive Homo Erectus May Have Survived Long Enough To Coexist With Modern Humans", *Time*, 23 December 1996.

17 S. J. Gould, *Natural History*, vol. 85, 1976, p. 30.

18 Solly Zuckerman, *Beyond The Ivory Tower*, p. 19.

19 Richard Lewontin, "The Demon-Haunted World," 71 Malcolm Muggeridge, *The End of Christendom*, Grand Rapids: Eerdmans, 1980, p. 43.

20 Malcolm Muggeridge, *The End of Christendom*, Grand Rapids: Eerdmans, 1980, p. 43.

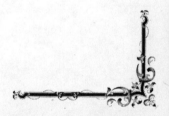

Goodword English Publications

The Holy Quran: Text, Translation and Commentary (HB), Tr. Abdullah Yusuf Ali

The Holy Quran (PB), Tr. Abdullah Yusuf Ali

The Holy Quran (Laminated Board), Tr. Abdullah Yusuf Ali

The Holy Quran (HB), Tr. Abdullah Yusuf Ali

Holy Quran (Small Size), Tr. Abdullah Yusuf Ali

The Quran, Tr. T.B. Irving

The Koran, Tr. M.H. Shakir

The Glorious Quran, Tr. M.M. Pickthall

Allah is Known Through Reason, Harun Yahya

The Basic Concepts in the Quran, Harun Yahya

Crude Understanding of Disbelief, Harun Yahya

Darwinism Refuted, Harun Yahya

Death Resurrection Hell, Harun Yahya

Devoted to Allah, Harun Yahya

Eternity Has Already Begun, Harun Yahya

Ever Thought About the Truth?, Harun Yahya

The Mercy of Believers, Harun Yahya

The Miracle in the Ant, Harun Yahya

The Miracle in the Immune System, Harun Yahya

The Miracle of Man's Creation, Harun Yahya

The Miracle of Hormones, Harun Yahya

The Miracle in the Spider, Harun Yahya

The Miracle of Creation in DNA, Harun Yahya

The Miracle of Creation in Plants, Harun Yahya

The Moral Values of the Quran, Harun Yahya

The Nightmare of Disbelief, Harun Yahya

Perfected Faith, Harun Yahya

Quick Grasp of Faith, Harun Yahya

Timelessness and the Reality of Fate, Harun Yahya

In Search of God, Maulana Wahiduddin Khan

Islam and Peace, Maulana Wahiduddin Khan

An Islamic Treasury of Virtues, Maulana Wahiduddin Khan

The Moral Vision, Maulana Wahiduddin Khan

Muhammad: A Prophet for All Humanity, Maulana Wahiduddin Khan

Principles of Islam, Maulana Wahiduddin Khan

Prophet Muhammad : A Simple Guide to His Life, Maulana Wahiduddin Khan

The Quran for All Humanity, Maulana Wahiduddin Khan

The Quran: An Abiding Wonder, Maulana Wahiduddin Khan

Religion and Science, Maulana Wahiduddin Khan

Simple Wisdom (HB), Maulana Wahiduddin Khan

Simple Wisdom (PB), Maulana Wahiduddin Khan

The True Jihad, Maulana Wahiduddin Khan

Tabligh Movement, Maulana Wahiduddin Khan

A Treasury of the Quran, Maulana Wahiduddin Khan

Woman Between Islam and Western Society, Maulana Wahiduddin Khan

Woman in Islamic Shari'ah, Maulana Wahiduddin Khan

The Ideology of Peace, Maulana Wahiduddin Khan

Indian Muslims, Maulana Wahiduddin Khan

Introducing Islam, Maulana Wahiduddin Khan

Islam: Creator of the Modern Age, Maulana Wahiduddin Khan

Islam: The Voice of Human Nature, Maulana Wahiduddin Khan

Islam Rediscovered, Maulana Wahiduddin Khan

Words of the Prophet Muhammad, Maulana Wahiduddin Khan

God Arises, Maulana Wahiduddin Khan

The Call of the Qur'an, Maulana Wahiduddin Khan

Building a Strong and Prosperous India and Role of Muslims, Maulana Wahiduddin Khan

Islam As It Is, Maulana Wahiduddin Khan

Sermons of the Prophet Muhammad, Assad Nimer Busool

Bouquet of the Noble Hadith, Assad Nimer Busool

Forty Hadith, Assad Nimer Busool

Hijrah in Islam, Dr. Zafarul Islam Khan

Palestine Documents, Dr. Zafarul Islam Khan

At the Threshold of New Millennium, Dr. Zafarul Islam Khan

Islamic Sciences, Waqar Husaini

Islamic Thought..., Waqar Husaini

The Qur'an for Astronomy, Waqar Husaini

A Dictionary of Muslim Names, Prof. S.A. Rahman

Let's Speak Arabic, Prof. S.A. Rahman

Teach Yourself Arabic, Prof. S.A. Rahman

Islamic Medicine, Edward G. Browne

Literary History of Persia (Vol.1 & 2), Edward G. Browne

Literary History of Persia (Vol.3 & 4), Edward G. Browne

The Soul of the Quran, Saniyasnain Khan

Presenting the Quran, Saniyasnain Khan

The Wonderful Universe of Allah, Saniyasnain Khan

A-Z Ready Reference of the Quran (Based on the Translation by Abdullah Yusuf Ali), Mohammad Imran Erfani

The Alhambra, Washington Irving

The Encyclopaedic Index of the Quran, Dr. Syed Muhammad Osama

The Essentials of Islam, Al-Haj Saeed Bin Ahmed Al Lootah

Glossary of the Quran, Aurang Zeb Azmi

Introducing Arabic, Michael Mumisa

Arabic-English Dictionary, J.G. Hava

The Arabs in History, Prof. Bernard Lewis

A Basic Reader for the Holy Quran, Syed Mahmood Hasan

The Beauty of Makkah and Madinah, Mohamed Amin

A Brief Illustrated Guide to Understanding Islam, I.A. Ibrahim

The Concept of Society in Islam and Prayers in Islam, Dr. Syed Abdul Latif

Decisive Moments in the History of Islam, Muhammad Abdullah Enan

The Handy Concordance of the Quran, Aurang Zeb Azmi

The Hadith for Beginners, Dr. Muhammad Zubayr Siddiqui

A Handbook of Muslim Belief, Dr. Ahmad A Galwash

Heart of the Koran, Lex Hixon

A History of Arabian Music, Henry George Farmer

A History of Arabic Literature, Clément Huart

How Greek Science Passed to Arabs, De Lacy O' Leary

Humayun Nama, Gulbadan Bano

Islam and the Divine Comedy, Miguel Asin

Islam and Ahmadism, Muhammad Iqbal

The Islamic Art and Architecture, Prof. T.W. Arnold

The Islamic Art of Persia, Ed. A.J. Arberry

Islamic Economics, Sabahuddin Azmi

Islamic Thought and its Place in History, De Lacy O' Leary

The Life of the Prophet Muhammad, Mohd. Marmaduke Pickthall

Life of the Prophet Muhammad, B. Salem Foad

The Most Beautiful Names of Allah (HB), Samira Fayyad Khawaldeh

The Most Beautiful Names of Allah (PB), Samira Fayyad Khawaldeh

The Moriscos of Spain, Henry Charles Lea

Muhammad: The Hero As Prophet, Thomas Carlyle

Muhammad: A Mercy to All the Nations, Qassim Ali Jairazbhoy

The Muslims in Spain, Stanley Lane-Poole

One Religion, Zaheer U. Ahmed

The Pilgrimage to Makkah, Sir Richard F. Burton

Principles of Islamic Culture, Dr. Syed Abdul Latif

The Sayings of Muhammad, Sir Abdullah Suhrwardy

Selections from the Noble Reading, Tr. T.B. Irving

A Simple Guide to Islam, Farida Khanam

A Simple Guide to Islam's Contribution to Science, Maulvi Abdul Karim

A Simple Guide to Muslim Prayer, Muhammad Mahmud Al-Sawwat

Spanish Islam (A History of the Muslims in Spain), Reinhart Dozy

The Spread of Islam in France, Michel Reeber

The Spread of Islam in the World, Prof. T.W. Arnold

The Story of Islamic Spain, Syed Azizur Rahman
The Travels of Ibn Battuta, Tr. H.A.R. Gibb
The Travels of Ibn Jubayr, Tr. J.C. Broadhurst
What is Riba?, Maulana Iqbal Ahmad Khan Suhail
Concerning Divorce, Maulana Wahiduddin Khan
The Concept of God, Maulana Wahiduddin Khan
Conversion: An Intellectual Transformation, Maulana Wahiduddin Khan
The Creation Plan of God, Maulana Wahiduddin Khan
The Fire of Hell, Maulana Wahiduddin Khan
The Good Life, Maulana Wahiduddin Khan
The Garden of Paradise, Maulana Wahiduddin Khan
Hijab in Islam, Maulana Wahiduddin Khan
Islam and the Modern Man, Maulana Wahiduddin Khan
Islam in History, Maulana Wahiduddin Khan
Islam Stands the Test of History, Maulana Wahiduddin Khan
Islamic Activism, Maulana Wahiduddin Khan
Islamic Fundamentalism, Maulana Wahiduddin Khan
Man Know Thyself, Maulana Wahiduddin Khan
Muhammad: The Ideal Character, Maulana Wahiduddin Khan
The Man Islam Builds, Maulana Wahiduddin Khan
Manifesto of Peace, Maulana Wahiduddin Khan
Non-Violence and Islam, Maulana Wahiduddin Khan
Polygamy and Islam, Maulana Wahiduddin Khan
The Revolutionary Role of Islam, Maulana Wahiduddin Khan
The Road to Paradise, Maulana Wahiduddin Khan
Search for Truth, Maulana Wahiduddin Khan
The Shariah and Its Application, Maulana Wahiduddin Khan
Spirituality in Islam, Maulana Wahiduddin Khan
The Teachings of Islam, Maulana Wahiduddin Khan
Uniform Civil Code, Maulana Wahiduddin Khan
The Way to Find God, Maulana Wahiduddin Khan
A Case of Discovery, Maulana Wahiduddin Khan.